MEMOIR RECOMMENDATIONS

Sonika has written a beautiful and courageous memoir full of honesty, wisdom and heartfelt insight. Her story is a witness to the strength of the human spirit to keep moving forward, despite any artistic blocks, towards finding one's voice within the world.

I was struck by the unique depth of Sonika's story and her ability to weave a tale of tremendous self-love, acceptance and healing. Her wonderful book filled me with hope, faith and love.

Sonika is a true artist, whose memoir draws on her many artistic forms of expression.

Whether you are an artist, or just wanting to "find your authentic voice", this book will move you and help you to reconnect with your inner child, who deserves to dance in joy again!

Amber Flynn
Spiritual Counselor

In her book, "The Soul with Two Voices", Sonika recounts heartfelt stories of her life with wisdom and deep reflection.

Having been raised by survivors of the Holocaust, and growing up under a cloud of criticism and suppression, she experienced many hardships, but emerged in the end with greater faith in herself and in God.

In reading her story, I am reminded of a quote from Elisabeth Kübler-Ross: "People are like stained-glass windows. They sparkle and shine when the sun is out, but when the darkness sets in, their true beauty is revealed only if there is a light from within."

This is a tale of how one woman found her light from within. Beautiful….touching…inspiring.

Barbara Tyler
Motivational Speaker
Lecturer on Goal-Setting and Habits for Success

Sonika's memoir is a poignant and tender story of the extremes of duality we encounter in our lives and within ourselves, as we journey towards the truth of our being.

As she explores different aspects of this duality – black/white, Jewish/German, authentic face/public image – Sonika comes face to face with the split in her own being, as she undertakes an intensely personal journey towards understanding herself and her life.

In doing so, she leads us back to our own connection with ourselves and that which is larger than each of us.

Her book is a beautiful tribute to the winds of joy and sorrow that have shaped her.

Stacia A. Topping
M.A. Spiritual Psychology, M.A. Education
Soul Provocateur

THE SOUL WITH TWO VOICES

One woman's journey to
her authentic self

SONIKA MARCIA OZDOBA

ISBN-13: 978-1515230793
ISBN-10: 1515230791
Published: August 20, 2015

Library of Congress Control Number: 2015913411
CreateSpace Independent Publishing Platform
North Charleston, SC

The author would love to hear from you.
sonikaozdoba@gmail.com

Cover art - Veil Between Two Worlds, a painting by Sonika Ozdoba
Writing & Editing Coach - Len Hodgeman (LenHodgeman.com)
Cover design - Megan Wood (TangledArtOnline.com)
Photographs - Diane Gysin (PortraitsByDiane.com)

DEDICATION

This book is dedicated to my Mom and Dad,
Rose and Nachman Ozdoba.

Thank you for giving me life and
for making so much possible for me.

I honor and thank you.

ACKNOWLEDGEMENTS

I would like to thank Len Hodgeman, my editor and writing coach, for his tireless efforts in helping me to make this book a reality.

It has been an incredible privilege and pleasure working with and learning from you.

I would also like to thank the many teachers I have studied with, in different parts of the world, who have impacted my life and taught me what I needed to learn.

Thank you for teaching me to aim for the highest standard of excellence in all I undertake.

Most of all, I wish to acknowledge my family and those friends who have been there for me with their love, encouragement and support.

This book is my gift of gratitude to you all.

AUTHOR'S NOTE

The book you are about to read has been designed and conceived as a collage.

A collage is an artistic combination of objects and materials pasted on to a canvas. In the same way, our diverse emotional experiences create a collage on the canvas of our lives.

In this book, the narrative serves as the black and white "story" portion.

The twelve poems, which are interspersed between the chapters, provide "interjections of color" that paint a portrait of my feelings at the time.

And the final component of the collage is the cover art, which is taken from one of my abstract paintings, "Veil Between Two Worlds."

This painting provides the visual vessel that contains and completes the collage about my life.

CONTENTS

INTRODUCTION

"You have it all and more to make it in this profession," proclaimed my voice teacher. It was June of 1993. I had made plans to go to Germany to audition for agents and fulfill my dream of becoming a world-famous dramatic soprano.

For seventeen years, I had worked as a professional classical singer, nine of those years as a chorus member of the Bern and Zürich Opera Companies in Switzerland. I now felt ready and confident enough to launch my solo career and fulfill what I believed to be my life purpose – using my voice to deliver a message to the world in the most dramatic way I could.

Then, in August of 1993, the unthinkable happened.

I, who had prided myself on being one of the most thorough and well-prepared musicians in the Zürich Opera Company, suddenly began to forget both text and music, and to fall asleep during performances.

In those first three weeks of the new season, it felt like an invisible hand was moving over me and slowly taking away my voice.

I remember standing on stage during my final performance of Wagner's "Lohengrin". Towards the end of the performance, I was unable to send any musical tone through my vocal cords. I realized with terror that this would be my last performance on that beautiful international opera stage that I had come to love so much, one which held so many memories of wonderful performances.

The following day, I obtained permission to take a leave of absence. I went home to my apartment in Zürich and sat alone in my living room, unable to move. All I could do was stare at the wall for hours, completely in shock.

Being "the singer" had been my identity for seventeen years.

Now, I no longer knew who I was.

After my operatic career ended, I was compelled to go on a very different journey, one that forced me to look inward and review the events of my life to find the answers to this inexplicable loss that I was completely ill-equipped to understand or fathom at the time. I realized that my professional, classically-trained voice had served, for many years, to cover and suppress my real voice, the voice of my heart.

It was time to take off the mask and discover the real person underneath, and only through writing my story was I able to make sense of the events that happened to me.

This is the story of how I came to discover the two voices in my soul…

LETTER TO GOD
by Sonika Marcia Ozdoba

Dear God,

I pray to you for divine guidance and ask that you clear the path for me to find the work you entrusted me to complete in this lifetime.

I have always known that you had singled me out for a specific mission, but I ask and implore you to make it clear to me where to go and what to do. I want to be connected to you at all times and ask that you remove my sorrow and my lifelong sense of disconnection from you.

I will study your teachings, but in return I ask you to be there for me always – till the day you call me back to you and allow me to live in the beauty and peace of your Eternal Light.

I have walked the distant hills for many dark days and I need you to open up the portals of light in my own dark interior world that is too oft beset with fear and despair.

Help me to find a distinct path, a clear focus for me to follow, and guide my steps to the door you wish me to open. Clear the sand and tears from my eyes, so that I can behold the glory of your presence in my life.

Cleanse me of all I no longer require and make me a deserving channel of your eternal radiance.

I thank you for this blessing called my life.

Sonika

LETTER FROM GOD
by Sonika Marcia Ozdoba

Dear Sonika,

You have been searching a long time for your roots, and I know how often you feel afraid to go down deep into those roots. But if you want your branches to reach as high as you dare to stretch, you must go as deep into the earth of your spiritual connection with me. You must continue the path of your own unique soul, even when it means leaving behind the shell of all you have believed yourself to be up to this moment.

Dig deep, Sonika, dig deeper. Open yourself to the inner truth of your own heart. For your heart is the only place on this wondrous, majestic earth I have created where you shall find the depth and majesty of your own truth.

Truth is not in some magic potion or learned book written by some erudite scribe. It is right there in your heart. Dig deep inside and explore the crevices and corners of your heart's deepest longings, for only you know what those longings are.

I have not created you to settle for a small and mediocre life. You can now allow yourself to have what you have heretofore prohibited yourself from having. I have entrusted you with a deep and sacred mission and, when you listen to your heart, that mission will become clear.

You are made to traverse mountains and valleys that present all kinds of challenges, but the biggest challenge I give you is to go down deep into yourself and discover the roots of your true identity.

It is arduous work, and I know how much you fear the journey, but the priestess within your soul must seek out the holy grail of your destiny and know that I will be there to guide your every step, and be your constant anchor through the wilderness.

God

GROWING UP IN ZIMBABWE
A child of Holocaust survivors

If I would have known what I know today, perhaps I would have done things differently. Hard to say – we make choices with the best knowledge we have at the time. On looking back, I came to understand that most of my life was lived from an unconscious motivation – I had absolutely no idea why I embarked on a path that often baffles me, but I believe that the purpose of my journey was to ultimately understand all the elements involved in those choices and decisions, and to move from reacting unconsciously to a full awareness of my specific way of functioning in the world.

Happiness was not the force that motivated me. My quest for truth was the relentless fire in my soul, the Holy Grail that I sought with the fierce and uncompromising passion of a warrior. But the journey to that destination involved much agony, and required that I release all the false images that enveloped my core self, to uncover and embrace the real, authentic person beneath all the masks I unconsciously chose to wear.

I was born in Salisbury, Rhodesia, (now known as Harare, Zimbabwe), to Polish Jewish parents who had emigrated to Africa; my father in 1938, before World War II, and my mother ten years later, after World War II. I was the youngest of three sisters. My two sisters were older by five and seven years.

In 1938, when my father saw the political danger posed by the Nazi regime, he made the decision to leave Poland. At the time, he had a wife and child, and his intention was to establish a new home for his family abroad.

He left his family in Poland and went to make a new life in Rhodesia, working eighteen hours a day as a tailor, making uniforms for the British Army stationed there. He became a property owner and a furrier, a trade that he learned from his South African friend Archie.

When the time came to send for his wife and child in Poland, he approached some cousins in our home town to lend him the fifty English pounds that he needed for their fare. They refused to lend him the money. The tragic consequence of their action was that his wife and child were caught up in the transportation to Auschwitz concentration camp, where they perished.

My father never forgave his cousins for not helping him in his time of need.

When World War II broke out, my mother was in Poland. She was in the Warsaw Ghetto and was subsequently sent to four concentration camps, the longest incarceration being two years in Auschwitz. During the course of the war, she lost her first husband, her parents and five siblings. The only sister who remained alive had emigrated to Israel before the war.

My father had worked extremely hard to prepare the house in Salisbury for his family. When the house was ready, he received a telegram from my mother, who had been smuggled out to Israel after the war. The telegram stated that she had seen his first wife and child being taken to the gas chambers.

In later years, I remember him telling me that, on the day he received that telegram, he closed the shop where he worked and went home to his new empty house. His grief and heartache must have been unimaginable, especially after learning that his wife and child had perished in such horrific circumstances.

It must have been the saddest day of his life.

The incredible part of my parents' story is that they had known each other in Warsaw long before the war, and my mother was actually the woman that my father had always wanted to marry. She had come from an aristocratic and intellectual family, whereas my father was a tradesman. Dad had always felt that she was "out of his league", and believed she would never consent to marrying him. So he chose to marry someone else.

On learning that my mother had survived the war, my father sent her a telegram, offering to send her a ticket to come out to Rhodesia, on the one condition that she agree to marry him.

So my mother, who had no trade, and no way of earning a living, took a chance and went to a foreign country to marry the man who became my father, and start a new life for herself.

That is the way my father came to marry the woman he really loved. I have always found it so poignant that they both had to lose everything in the war, before he was able to fulfill that dream.

I sensed that theirs was not a happy marriage. Although they worked together building their business, it must have been an enormous adjustment for my mother to leave the highly cultured world of Polish aristocracy for the rustic backwaters of Rhodesia. She had been an avid patron of the arts, frequenting concerts and theater events in Poland, and she made up for the lack of culture in her new homeland by learning English and becoming an avid reader.

From her, I inherited my love for the arts, and from my father, a love of working with my hands.

It was always a source of great amusement to me, as a child, when my mother would make mistakes in English. Instead of saying, "You cannot go out with every Tom, Dick and Harry", Mom would mix up the expression and say, "You cannot go out with every Harry, Tom and Dick". I was constantly having to correct her English, but we had lots of fun with her linguistic errors.

Both Rhodesia and South Africa had opened their doors to Jewish war refugees, and the large Jewish population in my home town of Salisbury was a wide mix of people from different countries and backgrounds, including Greece, Israel, Spain, France, and Germany. Most Jewish families had prospered and established successful businesses for themselves in Rhodesia.

Since Rhodesia was a British colony, the schools were run according to the British system of education. I was always so grateful for the classes taught at my school. English language and literature were highly valued, and in addition to learning correct spelling, pronunciation and grammar, I was exposed to a wealth of wonderful English authors and playwrights including Chaucer, Shakespeare, and many of the modern English writers.

I loved theater from an early age and acted in several plays during my school years. My parents sent me to speech and elocution lessons as a young child, and I enjoyed acting in plays and reciting poetry at speech competitions.

As a young child, I understood little about the political situation in Rhodesia at the time. Non-whites, which included blacks and "coloreds", were required to live in separate areas from the white population. "Colored" people in Rhodesia were the offspring of white men and black women. These children and adults were often looked down upon by both black and white social groups, and the effect of this exclusion was to make them feel completely outcast from society in general.

One of these "colored" women, Mrs. Sanderson, worked as a seamstress in my father's business, together with five black African men, who were taught tailoring and how to repair furs. Mrs. Sanderson suffered a double ostracism, being both colored and divorced. Government taboos did not allow us as whites to visit them in their homes and I had no idea where they even lived.

In later years, right before Rhodesia became independent of British rule and was renamed "Zimbabwe", my parents made the decision to emigrate to South Africa. After the emigration, my father would travel a couple of times each year from Johannesburg back to his shop in Salisbury.

On each occasion, Bero, one of his African employees, would be sitting at the steps of the shop, waiting for him. He knew intuitively when my father would be in town, without anyone informing him beforehand. He was one of many black people in Africa who had this acute and highly developed intuitive sense.

As a child, I was barred from mixing with black and colored children socially, and prevented from studying their culture and their music. I was not allowed to play with them or get to know them.

Yet, despite the separation, I grew up with a distinct connection to black people and strongly believe that my own intuition, as well as my love of silence and wide open spaces, was a direct influence of black Africa.

I resonated with their spirituality and deep connection to the land, as well as their love of everything natural. I also absorbed and was fascinated by their love of rhythm and music. A friend from Kenya once told me that I am built like a black woman, with a small upper body and heavy legs, and that I even dance like a black woman. African dance comes as naturally to me as the air I breathe.

In later years, my art work showed the deep influence of African art and masks, and the process of "unmasking the self" through collage, using three-dimensional masks, became a powerful way for me to understand what had happened to me at a deep spiritual and psychological level.

Black people in Rhodesia were by far the most natural people I have ever met, and years later, after I left my profession as an opera singer, I went back to my roots, wearing African-style clothes, braiding my hair, and doing African dance with a passion, in order to reclaim a part of myself that I felt had been taken away from me. I even went back to eating African food with my fingers, which has always been my favorite way of enjoying a meal.

I often wonder what happened to the people who worked for us, whether they are still alive or have perished under the most ghastly of present-day circumstances. In the same way that I felt I had no voice in my family, African people, at the time, had no voice in a system of government that was intent on suppressing their voices.

Perhaps that is why I identified so closely with their struggle. There was a direct correlation between their situation and my own situation at home.

And the split that later occurred in my psyche was, I believe, a direct result of the split that I experienced as a child in my home and in my own culture – the split between black and white, between primitive and "cultivated", between the external "image" and my internal reality.

All this became inextricably interwoven into the fabric of my own personality, causing deep conflicts and many questions that would be examined and understood only later in life.

My heart goes out to the families of the people who worked for us. At a time in history where genocide and brutality have become the norm in my homeland, a huge part of me grieves for their losses as well as for my own, and it is my hope, through telling my personal story, that I can shed some light on the deeper causes of this severe rift between nations and initiate some kind of healing in the hearts and minds of humanity.

LIGHT AND SHADOW

Rhodesia, as Zimbabwe was then called, was blessed with sunshine all year round, even in the wintertime. As a child, I remember so distinctly the beautiful lilac jacaranda trees that lined both sides of the street where I rode my bike to school. The trees would leave a carpet of lilac blossoms that covered the road, and create a canopy of lilac above my head.

We lived in a comfortable, four-bedroom house in the suburb of Avondale and, as a child, I used to spend most of my free time playing outdoors – biking, swimming at friends' houses and engaging in a variety of sports. I would walk around the garden and watch the bright yellow marigolds soaking in the sunshine. The marigolds lined the side of the house and garden, providing the backdrop for a large avocado tree outside my room.

Drawing was my favorite activity as a child. Being quiet and introverted, I lived in my own world and loved working with my hands. I was fascinated by structure and symmetry and tried to capture these in my art work. When I studied biology in high school, I learned to draw and copy diagrams to scale and was enormously proud of my drawings.

Years later, when the house in Zimbabwe was sold, my only regret was having lost those drawings on which I had spent so much time and effort. They had probably been stored at the bottom of my bedroom cupboard, lost to the world, as much of my art seemed to be, throughout my life…

However, our home in Zimbabwe was not a haven for me. Since both my parents had lost most of their family as a result of the Holocaust, I grew up in the shadow of their extreme pain and loss.

As a young child, I remember climbing up on a chair in the spare room one day and finding a book on the top shelf called "House of Death". On the front cover there was a picture of a Holocaust child behind barbed wire. Her sunken terrified eyes and emaciated body haunted me for years and, with all the ghosts and memories that the war left behind for my parents, living at home felt indeed very much like living in a "house of death".

My mother was often quiet and uncommunicative, and I can recall many times when she would sit opposite me at the lunch table, lost in silence and depression. The contrast between the sunshine outside and the darkness inside her soul later characterized and became a reflection of my own emotional journey.

During our lunchtime meals together, I would try to arouse my mother's interest in subjects I was learning at school, but she was completely numb and impervious to any attempt at communication. She lived under such a cloud of grief and sorrow that after a while I learned to just be quiet, obedient, and dutifully eat the food prepared for me.

I can remember feeling like a stray animal in my family – a lifeless doll that was there to be fed, clothed and taken care of. And in spite of all the creative gifts I had been blessed with, this lifelessness stayed with me even into adulthood, ultimately affecting my whole career as a singer.

The only things that made my mother come alive were music and dance. She loved to dance around the living room and sing her favorite songs and, later in life, when I became a professional singer, it gave her enormous pleasure to hear me perform songs from the Broadway musicals that she loved so much.

Perhaps on some level, I felt I could make her happy by singing for her, to help lift her out of her depression. But, as a young child, the shadows of her past were too deep and too traumatic for me to understand. Being a witness to her intense and overwhelming grief left me feeling powerless in my childlike desire to alleviate her sadness and depression.

We had an upright piano in the guest bedroom in our house and, one day, I began playing "Twist and Shout", a popular song at the time which I had heard on the radio. When my older sister heard me play the song, she ran to my mother in excitement, crying, "Mommy, Mommy! I think Maci has perfect pitch!" Maci was my childhood nickname, an abbreviation of my birth name, Marcia.

The name Sonika was a spiritual name that I adopted later in life, after my career in singing came to an end. The full name – Ma Alok Sonika – is Sanskrit for "Golden Light" and was an indicator of what I needed to search for in my life.

My parents were overjoyed to discover an "infant prodigy" in their midst and, in their excitement, arranged for me to have accordion lessons. But when the piano accordion proved to be too heavy for my five-year-old frame, eventually the lessons were abandoned in favor of piano instruction.

At that tender age, I did as I was told, and attended my piano lessons. But I did not enjoy sitting there, practicing scales and learning music that did not interest me. My love was popular and dance music, not classical piano.

Sitting still, and staring at the black and white keys of the piano, made me restless and fidgety. Zimbabwe had a glorious climate, with sunshine most days of the year, and I longed to be outside, instead of being cooped up for hours in the house, doing something that bored me.

As a result of this newly discovered gift, I was suddenly thrust into the limelight. For a quiet, dreamy and introverted child like me, this new and very public role was disconcertingly uncomfortable. My ability to play any song I heard on the radio caused me to become the focus of attention, and within a short time I was recruited to play for relatives and guests at every available opportunity.

On some level, I enjoyed this sudden influx of attention, but that attention brought its own repercussions. I very quickly became aware that playing piano and entertaining people was the only way my presence was acknowledged.

I was there to perform, to please others, to do what everyone else wanted and expected me to do. No one showed an interest in my thoughts, my feelings or my heart.

I felt I had no voice in my family and no say in my destiny.

I had one function in life – to be a performer and impress people with my artistry. In those early years, I learned that my talent was the only part of me that people were interested in, but once I had finished performing, they showed no interest in me whatsoever.

And in this way I learned about the fickle nature of friendship and the cruel betrayal of a family that sang my praises in public, but chastised me in private, each time I fell short of their expectations.

I learned about jealousy and envy from those who claimed to love me, but resented me for having a light that shone too brightly. And I learned the heartache of only being loved for what I could do, but never for who I was.

My art and my talent became my burden of betrayal, the cross I had to bear, the punishment I had to endure as a penance for being too gifted. And each step of the way, it was pounded into me that I had no say in my own life – I was there to fulfill my parents' dream of becoming a concert pianist. Any attempt to deviate from their agenda for my life was met with harsh admonition and accusations of ingratitude for all they had sacrificed in order to make that dream a reality.

And so, in order to cope with this situation, I put on the mask of the performer, giving the world what it expected, and buried my real feelings deep down inside of my heart, body and soul. My authentic self went into hiding and disappeared from view – until I could no longer find her.

Discounting my real and authetic feelings was my first step towards self-betrayal, and it was at this exact point that a split in my psyche began to develop.

Every Friday night, my parents would invite guests to dinner for the Jewish Sabbath and, invariably, I would be asked to play piano at the end of the meal. This became a weekly ritual and, most definitely, a family expectation.

Friends, in awe of my musical talent, would recruit me to be their entertainer at parties and social functions. As a child, I thought that I was at last making friends, but each time I was finished providing the afternoon or evening entertainment, they would move on to other activities and forget about me. I felt used for my talent, and then discarded like a piece of old clothing, a feeling that followed me for a long time throughout my life and career.

There was little sense of loyalty within my social circle, and I felt no real love or caring from those who claimed to be my friends. My sole function was to perform for them, and I remained silent and resentful, never allowing them to be a witness to the effects of their callousness on my heart and soul.

The increasingly hostile environment of my home created intense havoc in my emotional world, causing me to withdraw and simply do what I was told to do.

I became the puppet on display, the pretty Barbie doll, the mannequin in the glass window, on show for the world. And later in life, when I became an opera singer, the irony is that I simply repeated that childhood role, and became a pretty puppet for the world, on a much grander scale.

I turned that childhood performing role into a profession, where I actually earned my living by donning a variety of costumes and depicting a different character on stage each night, like a human chameleon, molding myself to what other people needed me to be and do.

With time, I lost complete contact with who I was. I became disconnected from my own needs, wants and dreams. I had no dream for my life, no sense of self, and knew of no other way to function in the world.

I recreated the same scenario from my childhood in my adult professional life and became the same lifeless doll I had been as a young child – without any core or inside feelings, like a forgotten shell lying on the seashore.

Later in life, when I went to Vienna to audition for music agents, David, the American pianist I worked with, noticed this lifeless disconnect in my singing.

"I have worked with thousands of singers and this is the first time I have nothing to correct," he said. "You know your music like a photograph."

"But something is wrong. We have worked for two hours, and you have taken an hour and a half to really connect to your voice. On stage you need to be present and in full voice from the very beginning. There is some kind of psychological block inside you, and you will have to get help for that."

He was the first person to notice the discrepancy between the person on the outside and the missing person on the inside. When I left his studio, I remember wondering how on earth I was going to fix a problem I could not see.

At the time, he told a friend of mine, who was also auditioning for the same agent, that "if she (meaning me) could find out what it is that is blocking her, there would be nothing to stop her from getting to the top."

It was the first time that someone had diagnosed a block in my psyche, something that was to manifest several times in my life as a creative artist. I was always grateful to David for having had so much faith in my ability as an artist. Yet the experience left me shaken and uncertain as to knowing how to find a solution for this kind of problem.

For many years, opera gave me the opportunity to express my hidden rage and grief through some of the most intense and emotionally dramatic music ever written. I followed my parents' dream of becoming a professional classical musician, yet at the same time used opera as a wonderful medium with which to express my inner rage towards them. In becoming an opera singer, I unconsciously attempted to get my needs met as well as theirs.

I played the role of the performer for 32 years, until one day, the inner child, who had gone into hiding so many years before, decided she had had enough of living in a musty cupboard as a hidden entity, with no real chance of being heard and acknowledged for her real feelings.

The trained operatic voice, which I had worked so hard to develop, was my "socially acceptable" voice, but it was never my real voice. Despite its strong, resonant and dramatic tone, my singing voice was covering and stifling the silent, screaming voice of my inner child that was desperately fighting to get out.

After seventeen years of singing professionally, the pressure of the insupportable conflict between these two opposing voices could no longer be tolerated within my exhausted body and spirit and, at the height of my career, I very suddenly lost my singing voice.

My inner child simply made the decision that she was no longer willing to be a puppet for the world, and she finally took a stand about her uncompromising need to be heard.

The power of that unconscious statement was so strong that it forced me to leave a profession I thought I had loved, and to go on a very different and much deeper spiritual journey, to understand what had happened to me, and to see the thread running through the fabric of what appeared to be a fragmented life.

Sonika Marcia Ozdoba

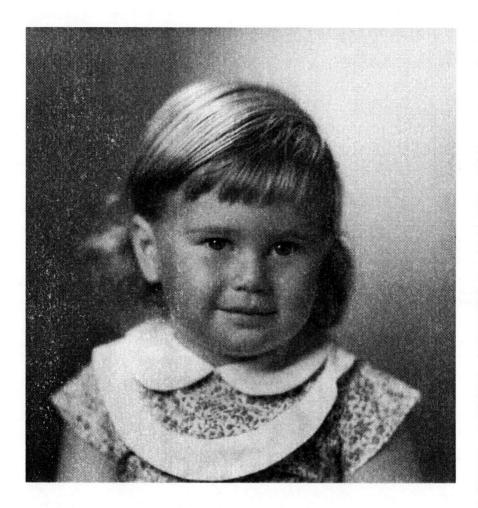

THE ONSET OF BULIMIA

In Rhodesia, it was customary for children, under the British school system, to complete two years of kindergarten. According to the school authorities, it appeared I was more intellectually advanced than other children of my age and, after my first year, it was decided I would skip the second year of kindergarten and move to a class with children one year older than me.

Once again, the course of my life was decided by adults, without my consent or participation in the decision-making process. I was too young to understand the reason for this decision, but on some level it enraged me that no one took the time to ask what I wanted, or whether I was in agreement with this decision regarding my future.

I followed along with their agenda as I was expected to do.

In a classroom of children one year older, I was pushed to perform scholastically at a level way above my capacity at the time. I often had to get outside help with certain school subjects, like history or mathematics, as I did not have the requisite knowledge or skill to understand topics that were too advanced for my comprehension level. In many ways, it forced me to develop and grow at a much faster rate, but my emotions had no chance to catch up with this situation.

Somehow, I managed to cope and actually did quite well during my school years. But the constant struggle to keep up with the standard expected of me caused a tremendous amount of self-doubt, and I never felt academically smart enough to compete with other students, especially the many brilliant and gifted young Jewish children in our community.

Despite adopting the mask of the "intellectually competent student", I knew in my heart that there were gaping holes in my understanding of many aspects of schoolwork and life in general. The image of being a "smart student" was a fraudulent front to cover up severe insecurities and lack of knowledge. I felt too ashamed to admit that I did not know or understand how to do certain things, and this shame around my lack of practical knowledge followed me into my teen years and into adulthood.

One of the most difficult aspects of life I had to cope with during those early years was my mother's incessant need to compare me to other young girls of my age. She had an obsessive preoccupation with my being slim, and insisted that I always have a good figure.

To her way of thinking, a good figure would lead to attracting the right man, and the right man would lead to marriage and happiness. It was what I called her "instant coffee happiness recipe" – get thin, find a man, get married and you would be instantly assured of having a happy life…

It was a recipe that, as you can imagine, did not sit well with a ten-year-old.

I could never understand why a woman, who had endured starvation for two years in Auschwitz, would be so obsessed with my having a good figure. My mother was

27 years old when she was taken to the concentration camps. I had seen photos of her at that age and she had been at the height of her beauty.

Later in life, when I asked her if she had been raped by the Nazis during the war, she denied it, vehemently. But some instinctual sense convinced me that she was lying. The trauma and shame of confessing the painful truth to her youngest child were just too much for her.

Her insistence on having a good figure made more sense to me when I saw it in the light of survival under such brutal and inhumane circumstances. Somewhere in her thinking, she must have learned that, if you had a good figure, at least you would only be raped by the enemy instead of shot, and this was the price she had to pay to survive, the lesser of two evils for a woman who wanted, above all, to hang on to what was left of her life.

It reminded me of the black women in war-torn African nations whose husbands would be shot by the militia if they went out during the night looking for food. Instead of sending their husbands, the women chose to go out.

They would inevitably be raped by the militia, but at least they could bring home food for their husbands and children. That was the only choice they had, to survive the cruelty of a country gone mad. Women will make such choices, when the survival of their family is at stake.

Even though I was never overweight as a child, my mother's insistence on being slim influenced my relationship to my body. Her constant comments about my friends' beautiful figures subtly undermined my confidence in myself and increased my struggle with weight and body image. Thus began a lifelong battle with comparing myself to other women, and always seeing them as more attractive and competent than I was.

Her comparisons undermined my confidence to such an extent that I assumed I would never have a chance at finding a decent partner in life or ever be "good enough" in her eyes.

Since the war, my mother's digestive system had never functioned properly, and at age eleven, I observed how she would drink a cup of senna tea every night to regulate her digestion. I began emulating her behavior by drinking a cup of senna tea after dinner, thinking this was normal in any family. But what began as a simple act escalated into full-scale bulimia, a debilitating eating disorder that wracked my world right up until my late fifties.

My addiction was compounded by my mother's decision to start educating me at that time about her experiences during the war. Every night, during our evening walk, she would relate all the gruesome details of her experiences in the Auschwitz concentration camp.

I was forced to listen to her stories for three solid years, until I could listen no more.

It is no coincidence that, at the same time she began relating her war stories, I began my own holocaust with my body and the bulimia. Whenever I tried to tell her about my suffering, she would counteract with the statement, "You don't know what suffering is." I felt that her voice and her story always had to take center stage, and my pain and suffering were minimal in comparison, having no value or importance at all.

My bulimia became a silent scream for help in a world where my own voice was not being heard. It spoke for me when I was unable to speak for myself or take a stand for what I needed. Since it was unacceptable to express rage in our home, my anger had nowhere to express itself except through my own body.

The act of bingeing and purging my food and my emotions with laxatives became a form of self-expression and provided some measure of relief from the intense emotional conflicts that raged internally.

Only later in life did I understand the true depth and reason for my bulimia, and the purpose it served. Although I often felt cursed by the affliction of this illness, my bulimia became, in a sense, my greatest and deepest teacher.

As women, we are taught that everyone else knows better what we should do, how we should be, what is good and what is bad for us. The media knows better, the magazine ads know better, friends and families know better.

We become afraid to trust ourselves.

Today I am thankful that I learned what many women are never taught – to listen and to trust my body. It is by far the most accurate radar system that I possess, and I have learned to listen to its guidance and its messages, even when people around me have a different opinion of what I should do in any given situation.

It took me many years to listen to my body and trust that my intuitive sense and my feelings would help me make the right decisions.

While studying at the Rhodesian College of Music, in my early years, I remember seeing a performance by four African children. They were playing marimbas, a kind of wooden xylophone – all with different rhythms, and dancing with enormous joy while playing at the same time. These children had learned to play music without notes, and their playing, in contract to classical music, made me come alive. I was mesmerized by their performance and their tremendous energy.

This early situation in life – being split between what I truly loved, and what I was expected to be and do – became manifested at a very young age – the split between the white and black parts of myself, between the authentic and inauthentic, between what I wanted and what my parents wanted.

In later life, this split made itself felt in the contrast between situations that truly energized me and those that completely drained my energy. My body, as always, gave me the signals I needed to discover the truth.

As I approached high school and continued to study music at the Rhodesian College of Music alongside my academic subjects, it became obvious to me that I was headed in the wrong career direction. I was physically not strong enough to be a concert pianist. My hands were too small and my arms and wrists too weak to manage the heavy, physical effort required for concert piano repertory.

My hands hurt from the muscular strain of attempting to master the heavy dramatic passages in Beethoven Sonatas and Chopin Preludes which were simply too strenuous for me, and I was slow at learning multiple layers of music notes.

I knew I was in over my head and knew that it was folly to invest my energy in a career that I physically could not manage. My small hands were made to work with more sensitive energies and art forms, like painting and writing. They were not suited to the heavy demands of classical piano pieces.

The inevitable day arrived when I was scheduled to perform a Rachmaninoff Prelude for a concert at the College where I was studying piano and music theory. The concert went disastrously for me. The muscles in my hands and forearms became tighter and tighter, and I just could not manage the piece. I realized in that moment that I would never be able to fulfill my parents' dream of becoming a concert pianist.

After the concert, my piano teacher passed the disdainful comment that I was a lazy student, and had simply not practiced hard enough. Both she and my parents were angry and disappointed.

I felt completely alone, with no one to hear my silent cry for help or to see that the level of performance demanded was impossible for me to maintain. Trying to maintain the facade of being a better pianist than I truly was finally came to a head, and my false image was shattered, once and for all time, at that concert.

Since my survival in the family was dependent on my being a star piano-player, I became terrified of what would happen, should I be unable to fulfill my parents' expectations. On some level, I believed they would throw me out of the house when I could no longer fulfill my role and my function in the family. I had so little emotional connection to my parents that it was natural for me to believe that I would be discarded once I had outrun my usefulness to them.

On that fateful day, I knew I would have to face my parents and tell them the truth. I could no longer pretend to be a pianistic genius, when in my heart and soul I knew this to be untrue.

I announced to them my decision to give up the piano. The consequences were devastating. My parents were beside themselves with fury, and their retorts tore into my sensitive heart and soul.

My father sided with and endorsed every accusation my mother sent in my direction, and there was no way to alleviate their anger. They were merciless in their reminders of how much money my musical education had cost them, and how ungrateful I was for all their efforts of my behalf.

I had shattered their dream for my life and despite my attempts to make them understand, their hearts were closed to me.

But I knew that I had done the right thing, and that this masquerade of trying to be someone I was not had to stop. I finally had the courage, for the first time in my life, to walk away from what I knew to be the worst possible choice of career for me. A career as a concert pianist would have been a completely inauthentic one, and I could not live without my own integrity, and without doing what was right for me.

Between the war stories, the conflict around my music, and my desperate struggle with food, life at home became unbearable for me. The atmosphere in our house was so suffocating and filled with talk of death that I could not stand it. Most especially, I could not take the constant blame, judgment and criticism I was forced to endure on a daily basis.

I began rebelling against every rule my parents made for me and this led to ongoing arguments about every subject imaginable. After giving up the piano, I could do no right in my parents' eyes. Every time I tried to express my own needs and wants, I was met with anger, verbal tirades and hostility.

My voice was shut down at every turn. After a while, this dynamic became internalized and each time a want or need surfaced, I shut it down myself and sabotaged it through bingeing and purging, a symbolic way of discounting and getting rid of my own wants and needs.

The denial of my voice, my needs and my heart built up a pressure in my psyche that became explosive. But being forced from childhood to live an inauthentic life is what really caused the most damage to my soul. The self-betrayal that had begun at age five became a life pattern that continued throughout adulthood and created havoc wherever I went.

Things at home finally reached a head, and I knew I had to find a way to leave a home environment that was stifling my creativity and my need to be myself.

Despite my parents' volatile reaction to the decision I made, I felt I had taken my first step toward an authentic life, my first step toward the Light.

EARLY DEFINING MOMENTS

In our home, as in most Rhodesian homes, we had three African workers – a cook, a gardener and a nanny. They lived in tiny dark rooms called "kayas", located at the far end of our property. There was one shower and a fruit and vegetable garden where they could grow their own food.

Since my parents were working all day in the business, they needed workers to take care of the house, the garden and the cooking. At the time, black people outnumbered the whites in Rhodesia by seven to one, so there was a large source of cheap labor.

People have often accused me of belonging to the "privileged white" class. In years to come, I often questioned exactly what that privilege was. It is true that black and colored people were not given the same freedom and privileges as we were allowed but, as a white child, I was also forbidden to go into areas where they lived, to mix with them socially, or to study their culture and their way of life.

At that time, the British (who had colonized Rhodesia) regarded the black people in Africa as primitive, ignorant and inferior, which in later years really infuriated me, because they understood nothing of the deep spiritual connection these people had to nature, to the land, and to life in general.

I have often thought that the British were so judgmental of the blacks because they were afraid of the "black" side of their own character, afraid of their instincts and their feelings. And I find it ironic that they gave themselves permission to sleep with black women and make them pregnant, yet at the same time denigrate them as a race.

To my way of thinking, black people were merely an outward representation of all the dark and hidden things the British feared inside themselves.

As a young child, I can remember standing at the gate of our house, waiting for a ride to school. Our cook and two other men were sitting outside the house, several yards away, taking a break from work. Three black women came walking down the street. One of them was substantially overweight, with huge bosoms and an extremely large rear end, while the other two were skinny in comparison.

As the heavy woman walked by, the men were totally mesmerized by her. They paid no attention to the skinny women because, in African culture, a woman who carries a lot of weight is a symbol of wealth and fertility. It shows that she is capable of bearing and feeding many children, in contrast to a thin woman.

Even at that early age, I was extremely conscious of the differences between black and white cultures. In my own culture, a girl had to be slim and if she was overweight, she was ostracized by her peers and by society in general.

I was astonished to see how much attention the heavy woman received, and was highly amused to see the nonchalant way in which she handled the attention. She showed no concern whatsoever for the men's opinions or comments, and merely laughed at them in disdain, leaving their tongues hanging out at the gargantuan sway of her sumptuous curves.

The whole manner in which men and women in black culture related to one another was so completely different to my own culture, and the vast differences between the two fascinated me.

But, in my home, the dynamic of living with three African servants was a difficult one. Being a sensitive child, I could feel the intense frustration and anger that lay beneath the surface of these workers, who were forced to look after white children and work in a white man's house for a white boss. They were forced to be subservient and to behave in a way that was expected of them, yet I can only imagine the rage and sense of injustice each of them must have felt.

My nanny, Anna, a quiet dignified black woman, looked after me while my mother was working or away on business, and my favorite memories as a child were the times we spent together on the back porch in the hot sun, eating the delicious African food she had prepared for me in a small metal bowl.

To this day, I can still remember the taste of her cooked meat and vegetables served over "sadza", the staple food of Rhodesia. Sadza was a grain very similar in texture to polenta, and when combined with meat and vegetables, it was, to my five-year-old mind, the most delicious food on the planet.

I would roll a portion of sadza in my tiny fingers and dip it the gravy, and feel like I was eating manna from heaven.

Anna's family came to visit her on Sundays, the only day that visitors were allowed. Her grandchildren were the light of her life, and that was the only time I ever saw her face light up. She had by far the sweetest grandchildren I had ever seen – tiny babies with huge brown eyes, and smiles as wide as the sea.

Once they left, Anna's face became quiet and without expression.

I can only imagine how difficult it must have been to look after a white child six days of the week, and only see her own children and grandchildren on Sundays. Yet I loved Anna like a mother, and there was a lot of confusion in my young mind as to where my allegiance truly lay – with her or with my own mother, who, because of her traumatic and painful past, was emotionally unavailable for me.

One day, while my mother and I were eating lunch, Anna came walking through the kitchen door, her face streaming with blood. Apparently, our cook had accused her of stealing some vegetables from his part of the garden and had made the decision to smash her face in with a bat. He vented his pent-up rage on her and succeeded in eventually causing her to go blind.

I was ten years old at the time, and when I saw my beloved nanny standing there in the kitchen with a swollen and unrecognizable face, something in me snapped. I went straight to my mother and told her: "Either he goes or I go.

I will not live in the same house as a murderer." Within two days, my mother got rid of him.

It was my first encounter with the kind of senseless violence towards women that seems to pervade our world, notwithstanding whether a nation is at war or not. Women often do not have the physical strength to fight off the attacks on their faces and bodies, and it seems to be acceptable in many cultures around the world for men to dole out this kind of abusive and violent treatment to them, be it through physical beatings or rape.

Nothing in my life makes me more furious than this assumption of acceptability. What these men do not realize is the irreparable damage to body and soul after such an act of violence.

I have no idea what happened to Anna, and my heart was forever changed by the image of her blood-soaked face. It took me a long time to truly understand what had motivated such cruelty towards this quiet and innocent woman.

Our cook was dismissed and my mother then proceeded to train the gardener in the art of cooking, while someone else was hired to care for the garden.

Another defining moment that stands out in my memory was the time I travelled to summer camp with both my sisters and got violently sick on the train during the night. I was convinced that our cook, in his rage against having to work for our family, had deliberately tried to poison my food the night before.

I was taken to hospital with gastroenteritis and then put on a train back home, while my sisters and friends went off to summer camp.

My mother left me alone in our house with my father and my nanny Anna, and left one week later on a business trip overseas. She did not have the time to make any arrangements for me the rest of the summer. I was left on my own at home, while my sisters and all my friends, except one, went on to summer camp. I felt completely neglected and abandoned.

They were all away for three solid weeks, leaving me almost in a state of solitary confinement, and it was at that point that something went wrong in my head. I was so isolated that I became severely disconnected from reality and was unable to function normally after that.

When my mother returned from her overseas trip, I asked her why she had not made any alternative arrangements for me to attend summer camp for the final two weeks. She replied: "It wasn't that bad, was it? Come look at all the presents I brought back for you".

I was taken aback that she had no concept of how her behavior had affected me, and in that moment, I made the decision that my mother did not care about me, that for her it was no big issue to have left me stranded for three weeks with nothing to do and no one to talk to. I was speechless at her insensitivity to my situation, and from that point on began to hate her with every fiber in my being.

I became the keen and relentless observer of all that was going on around me. All my anger and powerlessness became channeled into my eating disorder. I had no idea what to do with my rage, and that was the point at which my bulimia really took off. I began consuming huge amounts of food and unloading the feelings in the bathroom after taking piles of laxatives.

By some sheer miracle, it never occurred to me to throw up my food, as many bulimics do. God in His infinite wisdom surrounded my vocal cords with a sacred light of protection so that I was able to pursue a singing career in later years.

Later on in life, I met bulimic women who had damaged their vocal cords permanently from throwing up fifteen times a day. Their voices were hoarse and they were unable to even speak properly. I am so grateful that I was protected from that kind of irreparable physical damage to my voice.

Things eventually came to a head at home with my parents, and in 1972, on the advice of a friend, I applied for the American Field Service Scholarship to spend a year in the United States as an ambassador for Rhodesia. I was awarded the scholarship and went to spend a year with a Jewish family in Wilmette, Illinois, where I completed my final year of high school.

I was thrown into the limelight as an ambassador for my country and was overwhelmed by the demands of that role. I had been raised in a small and protected town, and coming to the United States at the age of sixteen was a huge culture shock. In general, it was not a happy or very successful year for me. I came back to Rhodesia in August of 1973, having gained seventy pounds in one year.

On my return, the next step in life was deciding on a course of study for college. The downside of growing up as a musical prodigy is that I was convinced that music was all I could do. I never believed I had any other option but to choose music as my career. It was what I knew. It was what I was good at.

And, of course, it was what was expected of me.

I applied to the University of Cape Town in South Africa and started my Bachelor of Music degree in February 1974, choosing piano and singing as my two practical "instruments". In my first year, I had wanted to major in musicology, a combined study of music and anthropology, but was not very inspired by the course of study offered at the Music College.

In my second year, I changed my major to composition, only to discover that composition was not really my strength. I had begun singing in the local opera chorus in Cape Town and was introduced for the first time to the recordings of Caruso, Gigli and Leontyne Price. I fell in love with the human voice and its power to convey emotion.

But I was becoming increasingly frustrated with my inability to find a focus for my career. Then a friend in the Cape Town Opera Chorus took me one day to meet his singing teacher, Adelheid Armhold, a 76-year-old German voice teacher who taught privately in her beautiful home.

In that one hour with Adelheid, I learned more about singing than I had learned in two years with my voice teacher at the University.

I knew in that moment what I wanted to do with my life. I wanted to become a singer and I had found exactly the right person to study with. Despite my parents' anger at my decision to change to singing as the primary focus of my musical studies, I was adamant about fighting for my voice, and for the right to choose what I wanted to do with my music.

It was the first time that I had refused to allow them to determine the direction of my life and my career. I pursued a general music degree in my third year and began private singing lessons with Adelheid.

Meeting Adelheid was the biggest turning point in my life. She was much more than just a singing teacher. Adelheid trained me and gave me the tools to become a professional singer, but she was also a symbol of the mother who finally gave me the voice I had been denied in my own family. It was ironic that I had to go over to "enemy territory" and find a German woman to give me my voice and to be heard in the world. Later I discovered that this was to become a pattern in my life, of going over to the side of the enemy, to get what I needed.

I knew on some level that my purpose in life was to get my voice out there, and was convinced that Adelheid was the person who would help me accomplish my sacred mission in life.

My encounter with Adelheid also marked the beginning of my spiritual journey. She was a devotee of Paramhansa Yogananda, and introduced me to the teachings of Krishnamurti, Helene Blavatsky, Rudolf Steiner and the ancient yogic masters. She also practiced daily meditation and was deeply connected to the creation and chanting of sacred sound.

In contrast to my previous voice teacher, Adelheid had a complete devotion to her sacred calling in life as a singer. Her spiritual approach resonated deeply with my soul and I became almost like a daughter to her, sharing many wonderful moments in her home, and learning so much from merely being in her presence.

I owe my seventeen-year singing career to this wonderful woman who gave me so much of her knowledge and her love for the human voice. After only fifteen months of intensive study with Adelheid, I was able to launch my solo career, at the age of twenty-one, as the soprano soloist in a performance of Handel's oratorio "The Messiah".

FORGOTTEN CHILD

by Sonika Marcia Ozdoba

My earliest memory
A sunny quiet day
And a child with no one to talk to
Hours drifting by
Time standing still
And a feeling of such
Desolation and abandonment

No one to hold her
No one to cuddle with
Questions in her eyes
Pain, such pain, in her heart
Unfathomable sorrow
And a sense of loss
Time drifts by and she loses herself

Slowly, steadily, but with no pity
A heart in a desert, searching
For water, but no water to be had
She slips away from life
She slips out of reality
And goes to a place
Where no one can find her

Safe and forgotten, condemned and unwanted
A testament of neglect
With no accountability
She slips away until she becomes
A shell, lifeless, loveless, love-deprived,
Condemned to live an agony
That no one sees or cares about

Forgotten by all, disregarded by all,
She slips away into her tiny world
Afraid to move, afraid to feel
Serrated by life's senseless cruelty,
She hugs her one and only teddy bear
But the bear is dead, just
Like her

THE START OF MY CAREER

The first two and a half years of my solo singing career were wonderful. In April of 1977, I sang Handel's "Messiah" with the Cape Town Symphony Orchestra and loved the feeling of singing to a large audience in a large hall. Music brings people together and is by nature a community event. As a performer, I met a wide variety of interesting people – orchestra members, conductors, soloists, teachers and professors, as well as many gifted students at the University of Cape Town Music College.

Music is a creative undertaking where each person involved contributes their specific talent to performing a work of art. I found it exciting to be part of such a venture, and especially loved doing it in service of something much greater than myself.

Although I sang chamber music, songs, opera and contemporary classical music, it was the religious music that I loved the most – oratorios, masses, cantatas, etc. I felt the most fulfilled when I sang music that edified God's creation. It spoke deeply to my spiritual side.

Classical music required me to sing in a variety of different languages. I loved working on the vocal technique for each piece, and mastering all aspects of a work of art. It was infinitely fascinating to me how different composers wrote for the human voice, and how it was possible to convey so much emotion in the melodies they had written.

The gift of perfect pitch made me an invaluable asset to conductors and orchestras, especially when performing the music of modern composers which was difficult for most other singers to pitch. These works were melodically and rhythmically challenging, but there was a great sense of accomplishment once I had overcome the difficulties of learning and performing them, either in front of an audience or later in a recording studio.

In August of 1977, I was approached by Professor Fiasconaro, Head of the University of Cape Town Opera School, to sing the role of Madame Lidoine in "Dialogues of the Carmelites", an opera by the French composer Francis Poulenc. The story was about the Carmelite nuns and I loved the role and sang seven consecutive performances that were very successful.

But the rehearsals were a different story. My previous singing teacher at the College of Music had been cast, like me, in a lead role in the Poulenc opera. This was the first time I was singing with her on equal terms as a soloist, which was a thorn in her side, considering I had made the choice eighteen months earlier to leave her for a better teacher.

It was obvious from the first rehearsal that there was great animosity towards me from most of the cast. I had been unwilling to settle for the standard of vocal teaching at the College and had "broken the rules" by stepping outside the box to find the best teacher in the business. As a result of my choice, I had come back with a voice that had been professionally trained by one of the best.

At one rehearsal, I pointed out to my old teacher an error that she had made in learning the music. I was ridiculed in front of the whole cast for pointing this out to her, but never again did she make that error in rehearsal or in performance.

She knew that I had studied my music with extreme attention to detail, and could not argue with the fact that I was right. For a teacher who had once accused me of being a lazy student and not working hard enough, she was now being uncomfortably challenged by someone who had an intense commitment to musical accuracy.

It was the last time she ever tried to humiliate me in front of other musicians.

I had always been fastidious about learning my work extremely well and made certain that no one could ever fault me on my music. My standard of excellence stood me in good stead through many future confrontations with other musicians during the course of my career.

In the final two performances of the Poulenc opera, my old teacher contracted laryngitis and had to cut a whole scene out of the opera, whereas those last performances proved to be my best ones. I felt very proud of my work and of the choice I had made to "step outside the box" and study with Adelheid. Her teaching provided a solid foundation that helped me throughout my life.

A few months into my career, I began having health issues and Adelheid recommended me to a naturopath who put me on a vegetarian diet. Dr. Oliver Lawrence was one of the leading naturopaths in Cape Town at that time and, through following his dietary plan, I lost weight and my voice and general health improved.

In the same way that Adelheid became a mother to me, Dr. Lawrence became a kind of surrogate father, and I found myself consulting him for advice about many aspects of my life, not just my health. Being so estranged from my own parents, I desperately missed having guidance about my career and life decisions, and I was grateful to have someone I could talk to.

Things were going well until July of 1978, when I gave a performance of Handel's "Messiah" in Cape Town. It was to be my last performance in that city. I began to have extreme abdominal pain and was having difficulty with the top register of my voice. It was alarming for me to realize that the whole top octave of my voice was not functioning properly.

I asked Dr. Lawrence what was wrong and why I was in so much pain. His advice at the time was to reduce the quantities I was eating, but I somehow knew that he had no idea what was really wrong with me. He had been an emotional support to me for almost two years, and suddenly I felt extremely alone.

At the same time, I learned that Adelheid was planning to leave South Africa and move to Hawaii with her partner, a man who had known her late husband. This was a terrible blow to me. I had always thought she would be there for me, and once again, I felt my "mother" was abandoning me at a time when I needed her most.

With my whole support system gone, I became extremely vulnerable and in need of some kind of anchor to hold on to. I believed at the time that once university was over, my parents would stop supporting me. In my emotional state of crisis, I grasped on to any support I could find.

One night, in June of 1978, I met a man at a restaurant. He showed an interest in me and, in my state of complete fear, ill-health and faulty thinking, I decided after a short time to move in with him and ultimately to marry him, without informing my parents or anyone else of my decision.

I had given myself no time to discover who this man really was and, on the night of our honeymoon, discovered that I was dealing with someone extremely volatile and violent. He started beating me and became insanely jealous when he thought I was paying attention to other men.

Things went from bad to worse and, when I ultimately went for a pregnancy test, I discovered that I was not only pregnant, but I had an ovarian cyst the size of a football that was within two days of bursting. The cyst was full of toxic fluid and, if it had burst, the fluid would have gone straight to my brain and killed me.

In a strange twist of fate, this unstable individual I was married to actually saved my life. If I had never gone for a pregnancy test, I could have lost my life, within days, to a ruptured ovarian cyst. It was amazing to me how God protected my life, even under such dire circumstances.

I was taken in for immediate surgery to have the cyst removed. My parents, who had heard through a friend about my situation, came to Cape Town to help me out. The pregnancy was terminated, on psychiatric grounds, a month after the ovarian cyst had been removed. I suffered a nervous breakdown and finally went back home with my parents to Johannesburg to recover from both surgeries.

All of this happened six months before graduation and, although I was in terrible pain from the six-inch cut down the front of my belly, my mother encouraged me to go back to Cape Town to study for my final exams. In her practical way, she knew the importance of having a degree to get a decent job, and so I went back to Cape Town to stay with friends and finish my degree.

The physical pain from the operation was so extreme that it took me half an hour to walk up one flight of stairs to the examination room where I wrote my finals. But in February of 1979 I was granted a Bachelor's Degree in Music and was able to finally leave Cape Town and all the sad events of that time to start over again in Johannesburg.

It took eighteen months for the scar from the operation to heal. Only then was I able to slowly start training again as a singer. After spending a year living with my parents, I moved into my own apartment and found a job working for the South African Broadcasting Corporation as Assistant to the Sheet Music Librarian.

I was responsible for cataloguing vocal scores, keeping track of accounts and helping orchestral musicians who came in to do session work. With time, I began giving concerts and doing some recording work for radio and television. I also joined a Jewish vocal group known as "Take Six", writing vocal arrangements of popular melodies for vocal quintet and piano.

It became apparent after a while, however, that there was no future for me as a singer in Johannesburg and, on the recommendation of a friend, I decided to apply for the Rotary Scholarship to study abroad for a year in London. My friend had been a Rotary scholar one year previously, and she was extremely helpful in assisting me to fill out all the necessary paperwork.

I ended up being the first musician from South Africa to ever be awarded the Rotary Scholarship, and left Johannesburg in August 1982 for what turned out to be two years of study at the Guildhall School of Music and Drama in London, England. I began my vocal studies with Vera Rósza and then went on to study with Rudolf Piernay, a brilliant voice teacher at the Guildhall School, who specialized in the French and German repertory.

While living in England, I stayed at the International Students House behind the Baker Street train station. The population of the student house was about 80 percent black, with students from West Africa, India, Pakistan, Sudan and Jamaica. I was the only white student from

South Africa and came up against a lot of anti-white prejudice from the black African students.

One night, after about a year of living there, my neighbor, a beautiful young woman from Ghana, came knocking at my door. Her name was Ada Ene, and she was a law student staying at the student house. She had cooked plantains for dinner and invited me to join her. Plantains are the staple food of Ghana and they were delicious. I was astounded to receive her invitation, since so many students had rejected me for being a white South African.

When I asked Ada why she had invited me over, she replied, "I wanted to know who this South African woman is who never talks to anybody". Being a withdrawn and quiet student, I was not aware that anyone even noticed me, but my lack of social contact had obviously made Ada question who I was and why I was not connecting with any of the other students.

Ada and I became good friends, and when I went for two weeks to Germany to audition for music agents, she did something for me that I never forgot.

During my absence, there was an incident where her neighbor from Sudan was threatened with a knife by a Jamaican student sharing her room. Apparently, the Jamaican student claimed that I was the person who had drawn the knife.

A general meeting was held at the student house with all the students present, and Ada stood up when my name was mentioned and acted as a witness to prove that I had been in Germany auditioning during the time when the knife incident had occurred. Without her testimony, I would have returned to find myself the subject of a court case, with a possible arrest.

I left England shortly afterwards and never had the chance to truly thank her for saving my name and my life. It was the first time that a black woman had ever stood up for me in my defense and helped me in this way. I was deeply grateful for her kindness.

As a foreigner, I had no permit to work in England, so after two years in London, I took Rudolf's advice and went to audition for agents in Germany. At every step in my career, what seemed like a door closing ended up being God's way of moving me on to the next phase of my journey.

At my audition for ZBF, a music agency in Frankfurt, I was offered a chorus job at the Bern State Theater in Switzerland and was advised by my agent to take the job and learn my trade while working in the chorus, before I attempted any solo audition work. At the time, I had no concept of what was involved in working in a professional European opera house and was very thankful that he gave me this practical advice and direction.

My friend Jenny, a fellow singer, asked her parents to help me out with a loan to cover the travel costs from England to Switzerland as well as six months of living expenses. Without her help, I have no idea how I would have managed the transition to living in Bern at the time.

Sonika Marcia Ozdoba

So after leaving England in August of 1984, I became a
member of the Bern Opera Chorus in Switzerland, where I
stayed for three years and did what my agent in Frankfurt
had suggested – I learned my trade, I learned about
working in a German theater and, most importantly, I
learned the language.

WAITING

by Sonika Marcia Ozdoba

The sunrise opens to a new day but at sunset I am
reminded that all is temporary, that all will pass, and I
have only today, to live to the fullest.

My home too is temporary, as are my relationships.
Only my spirit is eternal.

What will I make of this day?
What will I learn and experience?

Each day is a new beginning and each sunset is a new end.
Everything has its own cycle, its own ebb and flow.

I look to the Light and follow its glow.
I look to the darkness and listen to its silence.

And I look in between to the shadows and the veils of
life's mysteries and hidden treasures that lie waiting for
me to step into that place of the unknown.

I wait with reverence.
I wait with majesty.
I descend into the welcome arms of life itself.

Sonika Marcia Ozdoba

FULFILLING MY MISSION

For many years, as a child, I can remember feeling like I had no allies at home. Being an introvert, I had the tendency to make one good friend at a time, but those friendships were always accompanied by great fear and doubt as to how long they would last. I think this is the reason that I rarely stayed in touch with old friends, once I moved on to new places.

During my childhood, I had one friend who always felt she was in competition with me as a pianist and was only my friend when I was in second place to her. She made it clear to me that she always had to be first in everything.

So I developed the habit of putting myself in second place to keep her friendship, afraid that, if my light shone too brightly, I would be a threat to her and would lose her. This fear of outshining a friend, and causing unwanted jealousy, affected my relationships and my career. Other childhood friends were interested in my contribution as an entertainer, but few were a support to me when I really needed them.

Those early experiences made me wary of trusting that people would truly love and support me. When I went to London, Ada was my only friend at the International Students House, and Jenny was my one faithful friend in the singing world. I never became part of any community, but was always grateful to have one loyal companion with whom I could converse.

Another pattern that emerged over the years was that of going on a relentless quest for the best teachers. During my degree years at the Music College in Cape Town, I had the great fortune to work with brilliant teachers like James May, who taught harmony and counterpoint, and Peter Klatzow, who taught me the principles of composition.

But it was only when I started working as a professional singer that all my individual university studies of form, structure, harmony and counterpoint finally came together. I could now apply them to my singing.

As a student in Cape Town, Adelheid's teaching took my voice and my career to a whole new level. In England my studies with Rudolf Piernay gave me the solid foundation to do an excellent audition in Germany and to secure my first professional chorus job at the Berner Stadttheater (Bern State Theater) in Switzerland.

When I moved to Bern in August 1984, at the age of 29, I was faced with the challenge of working in a theater where I could not understand the language or read the rehearsal schedule, which was written in German. Once again, I looked around for a teacher and asked the Assistant Chorus Director, Ernst Hametner, if he would help me learn my trade.

Hametner was a brilliant teacher and he taught me everything I would need to survive in the profession – language pronunciation, how to prepare and edit a score, and all the practical tools of actually singing the musical material.

I put much more effort into my chorus work than was essentially required for the job because I was afraid of not knowing my music perfectly. Being a perfectionist, I was very exact about learning my music properly and felt a great sense of pride when I had prepared my music thoroughly and learned it well. Most of all, I felt a sense of mastery – of myself and of the challenge presented to me.

By setting the highest standard of excellence for myself, I caught the attention of my Chorus Director, Anton Knüsel. In my first year in Bern, we were scheduled to perform an extremely difficult modern opera. I am a visual learner, and could not make head or tail of what was going on in the chorus part, or how it fit into the opera as a whole. I decided to buy my own copy of the complete vocal score in order to learn my music accurately.

When Knüsel saw me underlining and marking a full score of the opera, he was impressed that I had spent my own money to buy it. I ended up buying full scores for every opera that we studied, and became an important musical reference point for many other singers in the Company.

When the time came for me to leave Bern, Knüsel found a way to keep me in the Chorus for an extra year because he valued the standard of my work.

The reason that I went to such lengths to learn my work was because I knew my own limitations and weaknesses as a musician, and I needed to feel secure in my ability to do the job well. The path to becoming an opera singer involves a high degree of self-awareness and self-mastery as well as being a constant and vigilant learner. I was very aware of the areas in my vocal technique and musical education that needed strengthening, and was extremely grateful that Knüsel and Hametner were there to teach me what I needed to learn about what is essentially an extremely complex art form.

Opera singing requires a high degree of intelligence and tremendous skill, and I used the time to learn as much as I could from these two excellent teachers.

The Bern Opera Chorus consisted of 32 singers from Bulgaria, Poland, Hungary, Rumania, Czechoslovakia, Germany, Austria, Spain and the United States. I was the only singer from Africa and the only Jewish woman in the Chorus. Many of the European countries represented in the Chorus had been actively involved in the Holocaust during World War II.

It took me a number of years to realize that I had taken on an unconscious mission to go back into "enemy territory" forty years after the war, to study the language of the enemy, and to work together under the same roof with representatives of those countries who had supported the extermination of the Jews during the Holocaust.

I had made it my mission to go back to the "scene of the crime", so to speak, to claim not only my own voice, but also the voices of all those Jews who had perished in the Holocaust, including the families of my parents.

My presence was a living reminder to the chorus members from those European countries that their forefathers had been responsible for participating in and contributing to the annihilation of six million Jews, and even though they had silenced so many voices, here was one Jewish voice that they would not and could not extinguish.

I was there to take a stand and I was there to stay.

Right from the beginning, I had to deal with a hornet's nest of extreme and hostile anti-Semitism. Many of the women, especially the Polish singers, looked for every possible way to get me kicked out of the theater. Their attitude pushed me to become the hardest working singer in the entire Chorus, and my perfect pitch became a lethal weapon that I wielded in my working with these singers.

In order to do their job well, the chorus women were forced to rely on my ability to pitch notes correctly. They would need to check my full opera score during rehearsal so that they would avoid making errors, and they were forced to stand close to me on stage during vocally challenging and modern operas, to ensure that they sang the correct pitch.

It gave me great satisfaction to observe their discomfort in having to work on an equal basis with a Jew, and to rely on her in order to keep their own jobs.

I had one good friend in the Chorus, Magda Radics, a Hungarian mezzo-soprano, who became my ally amidst a sea of hostile faces. She was the only one who knew about my two secret illnesses – bulimia, and epilepsy, which I had had since the age of twenty-five. Epilepsy would have been a valid reason for the management to dismiss me from the company as it constituted a threat to any stage production. Luckily, I never experienced any grand mal seizures while working on stage, and later in life, the epilepsy went away of its own accord.

The bulimia was a constant problem during that time and it was exhausting to sing professional opera while depleting my body with laxatives. To this day, I have no idea how I managed such strenuous and demanding work while hurting my body so relentlessly. Later on in life, I realized that the bingeing and purging was my body's way of letting me know that I was in the wrong ballpark, that opera was not the right career path for my heart and soul.

In spite of the very stressful emotional strain on my nervous system, I did enjoy many aspects of my work in Bern. Learning my trade and learning the language were both interesting to me, and I had a lot of fun during stage rehearsals. Memorizing the music and the stage directions and watching the production come to life after a great deal of hard work gave me a deep sense of accomplishment. The audiences in Bern were extremely appreciative of our performances and it felt wonderful to be part of such a huge team effort.

In a strange way, the chorus was like a big family, and there were always birthday celebrations and fun times that we shared with one another.

The women in the chorus had a field day with all the linguistic mistakes I made in my initial attempts to learn German. One night, we were singing an opera in German entitled "Die Verkaufte Braut" ("The Bartered Bride") by Smetana. The chorus sings to the protagonist Marie, and tells her not to be hesitant in her decision about choosing a marriage partner. In German, the expression is "Sei nicht verstockt". By mistake I sang "Sei nicht verstopft" which in German means "Don't be constipated", which caused the women to laugh so hard that they could not sing the chorus part. Thank goodness there were a large number of us in the chorus to cover up the gaps in the music...

Often, the chorus members used to play pranks on one another on stage. Among the singers in our group, we had a number of real "characters" who made the production much more enjoyable with the jokes that they would initiate on stage.

In one opera, where there was a banquet with an array of food, my American friend Jeff came up with the ingenious idea of bringing crunchy potato chips onto the stage and eating them during the soloist's main aria. He also left a banana peel in the middle of the stage, possibly hoping that someone would slip on it right in front of the audience. (Not a good idea!)

Another time, there was a swimming pool constructed at the back of the set. Jeff, who had to carry me across the stage in one of the scenes, threatened one night to throw me in the pool. Luckily for me, he did not carry out his wish. I managed until the end of the season to avoid being "soaked."

Initially I did not know what certain idiomatic expressions in German meant and my ignorance landed me in some embarrassing situations, where I made a number of very inappropriate statements, without my knowledge. Luckily, people were kind enough to correct my errors, and eventually I achieved fluency in the language.

My parents had moved to Johannesburg in 1976, and in 1980, my older sister had emigrated from South Africa to California with her family. Once a year, my parents would travel for a three-month visit to California, to visit my older sister and the three grandchildren, spend five weeks in Israel with my middle sister, and one week in Switzerland with me.

On one particular visit to Bern, my mother started to argue with me about getting married. We were headed for the train station on their way back home to South Africa. Her statement hit a nerve when she said, "I don't mind who you marry, even if he is not Jewish, as long as you get married."

I was infuriated. Ever since childhood, I felt that my mother had controlled every aspect of my life. She had decided what clothes I would wear, what I should do with my life, and which people I would be allowed to associate with. Her remark shocked me and I felt humiliated by her approach to a subject as important as finding a life partner.

In an angry response to her statement, I asked, "So it is fine with you if I marry anyone off the street, as long as I get married?"

I had worked so hard to find my own path in life, and felt that once again, she was stepping in with her need to control me. I blew up in anger. All of this happened right before the train left, and in this gigantic turmoil, I heard her call out to me from the train window, "We love you", but I was so enraged that I was in no frame of mind to hear her words or her concern for my future. I merely reacted out of old childhood wounds, and the anger stayed with me for a long time.

I continued to study and work at the Bern State Theater. Although I learned a great deal from working there, it became apparent to me, after the first two years, that there was nowhere to grow or progress in my job and I needed to move on.

God made the decision, once again, to close the doors on my time in Bern, and opened a new portal for the next part of my journey.

Sonika Marcia Ozdoba

MY HEART STANDS
by Sonika Marcia Ozdoba

My heart stands
In limbo through the stream of eternity
Through the phosphorescent night
Of solitude, spent breathing,
Where I feel nothing,
World-deadness,
And yet so much longing
With love unlived,
Plastered between sorrow and grief
Hidden between my face
On the boughs
Of a weeping willow
Beneath God's sky.

Sonika Marcia Ozdoba

ACCOMPLISHMENT OF A DREAM

Much of my creativity, especially in the early years, was focused on pleasing other people – what would make them happy, which songs they would like to hear, and what would impress them. It never occurred to me to ask myself what I *liked* to play or sing, what made *me* happy. It was simply my role in life, to be there for others as an entertainer, and to perform for them when needed. I had no other function in life. I had no personal desires or dreams that I could identify. I was never asked what I wanted, so I never thought of asking myself that question.

From a young age, I followed along with the choices made for me by my parents, because I did not think any other choices were open to me. Ironically, I carried over this belief into my professional life. I had no say in the kinds of operas I could sing, and had to perform whatever repertory was outlined for the season.

Some of the operas were exciting and interesting. Others were so boring that I was hard-pressed to stay awake during performances, and had to endure operas which had unutterably idiotic story lines and the most boring and repetitive melodies.

If I am truly honest, the only dream I ever really had was to get my voice out there. I felt that I had a message to share with the world and I chose opera because it was the most all-encompassing, emotionally dramatic medium I could think of to convey the intensity of that message.

I had no idea at the time what my message was, but opera gave me the chance to give full voice to the deep and volcanic emotions in my body and soul, and to express myself physically through movement on stage.

I strongly believe that all emotion is stored in the body and requires a physical outlet to express itself. I was fortunate that I had that opportunity to do it through working on stage with a multidimensional medium that included singing, movement, drama, story, self-expression and visual interaction with others.

The expression of feelings through my voice gave me a measure of release from all the emotional tension I was hanging on to, and served as a kind of catharsis from the turbulence in my soul.

Initially, I derived great pleasure from knowing that I was doing a good job, and I liked being acknowledged for work well done. But in my second year in Bern, my friend Magda suggested that I move on and audition for the Zürich Opera Chorus.

Bern was essentially a small provincial theater, where all performances were sung in German. Zürich, on the other hand, as one of the top ten international opera houses in Europe, had a much larger repertory and everything was sung in the original language.

In Bern, the season comprised five operas, one operetta (a kind of "light opera") and one musical. In Zürich, thirteen operas and operettas were scheduled for each season. There was a wider variety of repertory, as well as the chance to sing alongside some of the best singers in the world. The pay in Zurich was also double what I was earning in Bern.

After my audition in Zürich, something very interesting happened. There was a Polish soprano scheduled to retire from the Chorus in a year's time after thirty-two years of working there.

I was accepted into the Chorus after my audition, but my Chorus Director in Bern came up with some story about how I needed to stay one more year to fulfill the terms of my contract. This was a complete fabrication. His whole intention was to keep me in Bern as long as he could, because he did not want to lose a good soprano, and especially one who worked as hard as I did.

By some extraordinary quirk of fate, the Chorus Director in Zürich kept the Polish soprano's position open for me for a year, till she retired. It was an interesting coincidence that she retired after thirty-two years, and I was thirty-two years old when I stepped into her shoes to work there, a young soprano of Polish descent.

Things had come full circle, it seemed, and it marked the beginning of my happiest and most productive years in professional opera.

During the year before taking up the position, I purchased the thirteen vocal scores for my first season in Zürich and studied all the chorus parts with Ernst Hametner, my teacher in Bern, in preparation for my first year of work.

When I left for Zürich, I took the thirteen scores with me, all with a hand-written translation of the texts into English, the synopses of the stories typed and pasted into the front of each score, and all the chorus parts memorized.

I can remember the day when I registered for my first day of work and walked onto that beautiful enormous stage of the Zürich Opera House for the very first time. The child part of me was just overflowing with excitement and joy that she now had the biggest playground in which to express her creative self.

But more than anything, I felt an enormous sense of pride and accomplishment knowing that I had succeeded in working my way halfway round the world to be in this extraordinary place, and was thrilled beyond words to have the opportunity to work with international singers, orchestral players and conductors.

Both the inside and outside of the Zürich Opera House are majestic and absolutely stunning. As far as I can recall, there are red velvet seats, high ceilings and decorated walls, with room for 1100 people in the audience. The first time I sang on the Zürich stage, I was terrified of the prospect of having to project my voice so far and so high, but I became used to it and loved performing there.

I arrived at my first chorus rehearsal with a 550-page score of Rossini's opera "William Tell" which I had prepared and translated from cover to cover. The chorus singers were aghast and somewhat hostile at being a witness to all the work I had done.

But I had always been adamant about preparing my work well in advance, which gave me extra time to devote to other problems that came along the way, once the main work had been taken care of.

I remember how I was ridiculed for "doing a doctorate" on each opera, but, as in Bern, the chorus singers slowly came to appreciate the resource that I offered by having a full score, to help them learn their own music.

Although I made friends with a number of American singers in the Zürich Opera Chorus, I spent most of my time backstage listening and learning from the soloists. I dreamed that one day I would stand beside them as a soloist myself, and I learned much from observing their performances.

It was a very exciting experience to work in an international opera house. About three hundred people were involved in the productions, including an Extra Chorus who worked regular jobs and then came to help us out in the evenings. An Extra Auxiliary Chorus was recruited to either pose as guards or soldiers in a production, or to carry certain items onto the stage.

What was interesting to me was the attitude that the Chorus had towards these "outsiders." Many chorus members refused to associate with people outside the Chorus, thinking they were "below" us, but I was curious to know why they had taken on this kind of work.

Switzerland was a difficult place to find friends, and for many people, joining the Extra Chorus was a way to find social connection, meet other people and be involved in an exciting creative project.

Parents whose children were involved in a production could also spend time with their kids at the Opera House without needing babysitters.

The other prejudice I noticed in the Chorus was towards the stagehands, the men who put up and tore down the scenery for each section of the opera. These men were also treated as inferior despite their hard work. Often, when I was waiting backstage and began conversing with them, the women in the Chorus would throw disapproving glances in my direction.

I could never understand the kind of prejudice they harbored. To my way of thinking, each and every person belonged there and was necessary to making the production a success – regardless of what kind of work that person performed.

And once again, the ever-present issue of anti-Semitism reared its ugly head in the Zürich Opera Chorus. But this time, it was the German and Austrian women who started giving me a hard time.

Many of the foreign singers were irritated when these women pointed out their language errors, but I was enormously thankful to them for correcting me when I made mistakes in German. It helped me learn the language. I needed to be able to work and follow rehearsal instructions and, by conceding to their "superiority" in this way, I rapidly increased my fluency in the German language. When they saw the standard of work I brought to the table, they became less critical. But underneath the surface, the anti-Semitism was always there.

The odd thing is that I had an enormous respect for the German women. They were amongst the most capable and knowledgeable women I had ever met. They knew the ins and outs of insurance, money management, the union laws, and everything that was going on politically.

They were also marvelous cooks and dressed impeccably, taking meticulous care of their clothing. Despite their hostile attitude towards me, my sense of humor helped me to bond with them, and we had lots of fun times, while learning what we needed to do for a production.

On one occasion, I was helping the women out with the chorus part of "Peter Grimes", an opera by the English composer Benjamin Britten. "Peter Grimes" was a particularly difficult score for us to learn and memorize.

The chorus members make up the village folk who are all against Peter Grimes, believing that he was responsible for the death of a young boy in the village. The hatred of the villagers for Peter Grimes was captured brilliantly in the chorus part, and it amused me greatly to see that, once the chorus members had expressed all their pent-up rage through the music, they suddenly became friendlier to one another and looked much happier than at any other time!

Getting all the anger out of the way seemed to free them up to become like children in a playground, where they could all just play with one another and have fun. The extraordinary result was that, in spite of our differences, this emotional release led to a feeling of bonding among the chorus members, and "Peter Grimes" became my favorite opera production.

During one summer, we were scheduled to perform Puccini's "Turandot" in the famous "Hallenstadion," a sports arena in Zürich. The Chorus had to climb hundreds of stairs behind the stage in order to reach different levels of the set, to enable us to see the conductor. I felt like a football player at the time, running up and down, backwards and forwards, to get to different parts of the stage, but I loved the music, and have wonderful memories of that production.

There were, however, other incidents that were less fortunate. One time, the stagehands forgot to put a security rope around a hole in the stage, and, during rehearsal, one of the tenors in the Chorus fell sixteen feet into that hole, breaking seven ribs, both collarbones and both wrists. Five weeks after the accident, he was back at the opera, ready to sing, with bandages all around his body.

I had tears in my eyes as I watched him sing his heart out with seven broken ribs, but marveled at the degree of commitment this man had to his craft.

His girlfriend was one of the soloists in that production. She had been with him in the hospital until 4:00 am and came to rehearsal at 10:00 am the same morning, ready to work, in spite of the terrible shock of his accident. It was three days before opening night, and being the true professional that she was, she was there right on time to do her job.

Zürich was a real education for me in learning about what being a professional singer is all about. "The show must go on" was a principle that the soloists modeled for me, and I was humbled to be a witness to such dedication and true professionalism.

My six years in Zürich, from 1987 to 1993, were truly a wonderful time. Although my main work was singing in the Opera Chorus, I was offered a few small operatic roles at the Opera House, and also did some solo soprano performances in local churches and concert halls.

But during the last two years, a change began to take place in me. It was to be the precursor to a series of events that totally changed my life and sent me hurtling full throttle into the dark night of my own soul.

Sonika Marcia Ozdoba

SOUNDS OF THUNDER
by Sonika Marcia Ozdoba

Sounds of thunder
Sounds of nothingness
Cannon-fire darkening my ears
And swords cutting through the air
With relentless harsh strokes

The voices drown out the night air
I long for an untenable repose
The cracking of whips and broken glass
Heralding the end of an unwanted era

How I long for the clink of glass
Filled with long-stemmed champagne bubbles
Tanks mow down the green lawns
Of my verdure-drenched solitary heart

And sleep calls me like a drug
To numb unwanted memories of feelings
In a place that has left me haunted
Deep do I lie in that soft place
With sounds that beckon from the hedgerows

Sonika Marcia Ozdoba

THE CHANGE BEGINS

During my time in Zürich, I received the news in 1991 that my father had passed away, and went back to South Africa for the funeral. The last time I had seen Dad was when he and my mother had visited me in Zürich. The trip had not gone well and had ended, yet again, in another argument. I had flown into a rage about some small thing they had done, and from that point on, felt that my father gave up on the possibility of ever doing anything right in my eyes.

In many ways, we were very much alike, but whenever there was a conflict, he always sided with my mother, and I felt no emotional support from him. I was hurting so much from all the conflicts that had occurred between us that it was difficult for me to feel compassion for him at the time.

It is a source of great sadness to me that I never had the chance to make an amends to my father for my volatile and unkind behavior towards him. He had worked so hard to support his family and always put his own loss and suffering in second place to my mother's. One night, in September 1991, he merely fell asleep and never woke up again, and I was grateful that he did not have to endure a long period of illness before passing away.

On returning to Zürich, I went straight back to work. I had found an apartment in one of the most beautiful areas in the city, only five minutes' walk from both the Opera House and Lake Zürich. All the shops that I frequented were close by, and I was earning enough money to furnish a beautiful apartment. My job was the highest paid chorus job of any opera house in Europe with an added bonus of six weeks' paid vacation during the summer.

However, at a time when I should have been the happiest, my bulimia escalated out of all proportion, and I was taking twelve to eighteen laxative tablets a night. Opera is a profession that requires intense physical work, emotional and mental strength, and enormous stamina.

I have no idea how my body managed to put up with that kind of merciless self-punishment. Yet somehow I found the energy to do my work in spite of this debilitating addiction.

Ultimately, the intense conflict of body and soul began to take its toll on me physically as well as psychologically. My body was trying desperately to talk to me, but I was not listening.

During those two years, I started to become aware of certain aspects of the music industry that disturbed me, especially in its treatment of women in the opera world.

As chorus women, we were silently looked down upon and regarded with ridicule, even though many of us were highly educated and had university degrees. No one knew or cared about our accomplishments, and oftentimes men would regard us as dumb, pretty "chorus girls" whose only purpose was to provide them with sexual favors.

Their behavior towards us was degrading and disrespectful in the extreme and made me highly resentful. We were mocked and looked upon as stupid, yet none of these men considered how much hard work and intelligence it took to be able to memorize and sing operas in Italian, German, French and Russian on four consecutive nights in one week of performances.

None of them knew that, in addition to studying the chorus part of Tchaikovsky's "Eugene Onegin" in Russian, I had also studied the entire 82-page solo soprano role in the opera, which I had learned, on my own, in Russian – certainly not the feat of a brainless "chorus girl."

There was also a great deal of ridicule towards the women soloists who were overweight. People would constantly laugh at them for needing to wear outsize clothing. These women had to work unbelievably hard to maintain the standards that were demanded from the profession. They lived out of hotels and planes and trains, traveling from one city to another, with no structure, no time to rest, and no chance of leading a balanced life.

They ended up becoming obese, to cope with the intense loneliness of their lifestyle. The insensitive harshness with which they were treated was insufferable, and made me question, for the first time, whether I was strong enough to deal with that kind of emotional cruelty.

As time progressed, and singing in the Chorus became my day-to-day life, I found myself slipping more and more into the shadows. No one knew how hard I worked. No one except me cared about the hours of preparation. They had no idea how desperate I was to be acknowledged for my efforts. I was one of many – unheard, invisible and unrecognized. As I blended into a faceless crowd, the voice I had worked so hard to develop became lost in a sea of voices.

I had invested all this money, work and time in my career and, after obtaining a position in the Zürich Opera Chorus, with its job security and excellent benefits, there was nowhere to go and no hill to climb. I had my beautiful apartment, an excellent salary, and had arrived at a destination where no further career growth was possible.

With time, the work became routine and the constant repetition of certain operas became an excruciating bore. I grew tired of giving so much of myself and receiving so little recognition in return. In the theater world, a chorus singer eventually becomes like a fly on the wall. No one sees you or respects your work. You just become part of a "singing machine", and I began to feel chronically burned out, both physically and emotionally.

There were constant arguments between the Chorus and the management about pay and work conditions, and the ongoing strife became a drain on my sensitive nervous system. I was growing weary of the negative atmosphere that constituted a part of my daily work experience.

Although there were operas that were exciting and fun to perform, the lack of personal fulfilment and the feeling of stagnation in the Chorus began to affect me emotionally. I felt that the more roles I slipped into on stage, the more split off I became from the core essence of who I was.

Having given all my energy to my career and none towards my personal life, I had simply repeated the pattern from childhood of putting my needs and wants so far in the background that I ceased to exist, except as a Barbie doll on stage, looking pretty, but with no self at the center.

The other areas of my life – like personal relationships, going out with friends, being part of a community, developing a spiritual life – were all neglected and not even considered important. After a while, I just became a shadow of myself.

To the outside world, I projected the persona of a powerful artist who had worked her way round the world to make it to the Zürich Opera House – a journey that had entailed drive, persistence and immensely hard work. But behind that successful "image" was a child in such despair and so isolated from warmth, love, and caring, that when each opera season was over, and the holidays came, she slipped into unreality and had no idea what to do with her time.

That experience of abandonment from my childhood, when my mother left me for three weeks, became the same place I went to in my emotional world, once I was left on my own, and that feeling haunted my spirit for a long time.

The fear of people finding out about my bulimia and my epilepsy caused me to distance myself from potential friends in the Chorus, until one day, they just stopped extending themselves to me on a social level. I became more and more isolated and disconnected from life.

During my last two years, an orchestral member who was dating a friend of mine in the Chorus later made a remark to me that paints a picture of what was happening on an internal level. "You were there, but you were not there." My body was on the stage, going through the motions, but my spirit was elsewhere.

Yet somewhere in my heart there was still the dream of becoming a dramatic soprano with a message to give to the world. In my final year, I put myself on a strict diet, exercised daily and stopped the laxatives for a whole year. Believing myself to be finally free of the bulimia, I felt I was ready to launch a solo career and began preparing my audition program for agents in Germany.

In July of 1993, I spent the summer on the Greek island of Corfu at a meditation retreat center and was introduced to the teachings of the controversial Indian guru, Bhagwan Shree Rajneesh. I loved the place and loved learning about meditation, but it took me a full five weeks to recover physically from the previous opera season.

On my return from Greece, the internal change began to accelerate and I was to know a kind of spiritual death and hell that lasted for a very long time.

LONGING
by Sonika Marcia Ozdoba

Inside this aching body
There is a soul

Inside this aching soul
There is a woman

Inside this aching woman
Is a body aching to connect

With something that was lost
Lost in the distant past

A life thrown asunder
By a lack of care and understanding

How to retrieve lost time
How to rewrite the story
Of a life that has not yet begun

A journey that wants to write itself
A longing for something not yet seen

To feel what is real –
To find what is true –
True for me

Sonika Marcia Ozdoba

DESCENT INTO HELL

The body is a miraculous guide and clue as to what is happening in our emotional world, and nowhere was the split between my inner child and my adult self so apparent as it was in the battle that waged between these two disconnected parts of my psyche.

My real self, the inner child, had gone into hiding at a very early age, because she had felt it was unsafe to reveal herself. Throughout my career as a singer, she found all kinds of ways to send me signals, when she felt that her needs were not being acknowledged, valued or taken seriously.

The most violent way that my inner child communicated her presence to me was with my bulimia and through the battle with my voice. Although she had gone into hiding to survive in the family, my inner child had been knocking continuously on the door of that proverbial "closet in the basement," where she had been relegated to live.

She was determined to beat down that door with all her force, in order to be heard from her intolerable place of imprisonment.

One of the major career obstacles I had encountered was a tremendous difficulty in being able to "move the voice". Singers of all types are required to be able to sing "coloratura" passages (runs and scales), and although I was able to sing long extended lines of melody, my vocal agility was a constant struggle for me.

Over the years, I came to understand that the tightness or block in the voice was my inner child fighting at the gate of my vocal cords, trying desperately to push through my singing voice in order to be heard. She kept fighting and creating an ongoing tension with my performing voice, because that suffocating "mask" was blocking her authentic expression.

With time, the tension between the two voices, the "mask" entertainer voice above and the desperate, screaming child voice below, became so intense, that my inner child finally broke through the thick wall between the voices with the relentless and uncompromising force of a volcano that had lain buried and dormant for far too long.

Her rage at being neglected for so many years finally shattered my singing voice, and forced me to give her my absolute and undivided attention.

I was completely unaware of this internal drama happening at a deeply unconscious level. But at the beginning of the new opera season in August of 1993, this unconscious drama began to slowly reveal itself.

The new Opera Director had scheduled three Verdi and three Wagner opera performances in the first week of the season. These operas required a great deal of heavy and dramatic singing and were extremely demanding for the Chorus.

As the season commenced, something began to happen to me that had never occurred before. I began forgetting my texts and would fall asleep from exhaustion during the course of the performances. After our morning rehearsals, I would need to go home and sleep for three hours. It was unusual for me to be that tired at the beginning of a new season of work.

Within those first three weeks, my vocal cords slowly began shutting down. I can only describe it as a kind of "energy phenomenon", as though an invisible hand swept over me and began to anaesthetize my singing voice. After ten minutes of doing vocal warmups, suddenly no musical tone was able to manifest through my vocal cords.

At the end of those three weeks, I knew that I would have to stop working for a while. My Chorus Director was extremely understanding of my situation, and after what I knew would be my final performance of Wagner's "Lohengrin," I took a three-month leave of absence and went to India, in search of my soul.

The shock of losing my voice was like no other shock I had ever experienced. I did not merely lose my voice. I felt I had lost my identity, my mission in life, my career, my community, and my way of earning a living.

But most importantly, I lost myself and my life purpose. I had always defined myself as "the singer", and without that identity, I no longer knew where I belonged.

For years I had been convinced that getting my voice out to the world through the medium of opera was the work I was meant to do in life. Now, suddenly, I had lost my compass and was sailing adrift on an ocean with no destination, no anchor, and no place to land. I felt like someone had hit me with a two-ton truck, and my whole body was in excruciating pain from all the broken bones.

After spending five weeks in India at an ashram (a religious commune) in Poona, I came back home to Switzerland and began intensive therapy with a disciple or "sannyasin" of Bhagwan Shree Rajneesh, whose teachings had had such a profound influence on my thinking and my spiritual life.

When my therapist made the prediction that I would leave the opera, I adamantly stated that I would never leave my profession. It was everything I had worked for. But as I started to examine the deep-seated motives for having chosen to go into an operatic career, I slowly began to get a better understanding of myself.

I was forced to face some very hard questions and to ask myself whose voice I had been truly fighting for:

Was I fighting for my mother by giving voice to the feelings she had never had a chance to express?

Was I fighting for the voices of the Jews who had lost their lives in the Holocaust?

Or was I fighting for the right to my own voice that had been so discounted and invalidated within my own family?

What exactly was the mission I had chosen to undertake, from deep within my soul, and why had God decided to take me out of my profession at the point when I felt ready to embark on a solo career? These were the questions that haunted me day and night, and I was desperate in my search for answers.

As an artist, I had grown to love the operas of Richard Wagner and Richard Strauss, only to learn later that these two composers, who were greatly loved and revered by Hitler, were also the most vehemently anti-Semitic composers of their generation. It had been a dream of mine to sing the dramatic soprano roles in the operas of these two composers, until one day I realized that, if I had achieved my "dream", I would have been singing in places like Bayreuth, the opera house where Wagner's operas are performed each summer. Some of the chorus members I knew were avid Nazi supporters and used to sing in the Bayreuth Chorus during the summer.

As a young Jewish dramatic soprano, whose family had perished in the Holocaust, I would be singing Hitler's favorite music and entertaining surviving supporters of the Nazi regime. As a Jew, the thought of "entertaining Nazi audiences" made my blood run cold.

I would have sold my soul to the Devil.

It was impossible for me to imagine how my parents would have felt if they knew where I was singing, and for whom, and it was just as unthinkable to consider the spiritual and emotional damage it would have done to me as a person.

But the question that I was confronted with, more than any other, was why I had even chosen to become an opera singer in the first place. As a child, classical music had never been my true passion. I found it boring and formal in contrast to the alive and electric dance rhythms of African and popular music.

Classical music, and becoming a concert pianist, had been my parents' dream, so I had initially tried to follow what they had expected and wanted me to do. I had fought for the right to have a voice, yet ironically my voice was still enveloped by the restraints and rules of classical music.

Despite my parents' objections, I had succeeded in my pursuit of a singing career, but it was still within the classical framework of what my parents wanted, and even though I tried to meet both their needs and my own needs, my voice ended up not being heard, and the medium I chose ultimately turned out to be an inauthentic one.

The stories I sang about in operas were other people's stories.

They were not *my* story.

I had pursued my "dream," but I had sadly compromised myself in the process.

As a chorus singer, my voice was not respected or taken seriously, and this was an exact repetition of the feeling I had had in childhood. At the end of seventeen years of backbreaking work, I had poured all my energy into a thankless profession, where I received no personal appreciation or recognition for my efforts.

Perhaps the most baffling and disturbing element of my past was the fact that from the very beginning of my career, I had made the decision to go over into "enemy territory". I studied my craft with two German voice teachers, made my living in two German-speaking opera houses, and learned the German language fluently.

Since I had felt used and rejected by my own Jewish community in Zimbabwe, I remedied that rejection by going over to the enemy camp. I found German-speaking friends in Europe and worked hard for artistic acceptance in enemy territory. I found a German "mother-figure", Adelheid, to give me a voice, when my own mother had not given credence to my voice or my feelings at home.

From early on in my life, I felt that my mother had held the power and control over my life. She had often commented that without her financial support, I would never have made it as a singer. I felt she always held the final card – control over the money – and therefore over my success and my career. Every success I had was interpreted as her personal success and, in the end, I felt she claimed all the credit for my hard-earned achievements as a musician.

Her story and her suffering had always taken center stage in my home, and since my own voice was continually shut down in my family, opera gave me the chance to at last take center stage in my own drama. I desperately needed to be heard and to receive recognition and attention for my own suffering.

There came a defining moment, however, when the child in me became unwilling to allow my mother to claim ownership and power over my life, the way I felt she had done for so many years.

Every day of her life, the child in me had fought an ongoing battle against the tyranny of my mother's voice, determined to be the winner and reign victorious, to claim her life as her own, and to live it on her own terms.

And so, with the inherent genius that exists in every child's heart, she devised a way to shut down her own voice, so that my mother would never again lay claim to her voice, or determine the course of her own life. My inner child withdrew her gift from the world, to prevent that gift being raped and stolen from her.

With all her force and passion, the child in me hung on to the one thing she would not allow my mother to take away from her, the one thing she knew was hers and hers alone – her voice. Like a favorite teddy-bear that she would have saved from the flames of a burning house, the child in me grabbed the one possession she loved and valued the most, and ran from a lifestyle and a mother whose agenda was strangling and suffocating her very existence on the planet.

She had followed, on some level, what her mother wanted her to do, and then had to deal with those two conflicting aspects of love and hatred, loyalty and rage, and light and shadow in her own being that created such inner turmoil and provided the wellspring for such a multifaceted outpouring of creative energy.

Yet the sad and ironic truth is that, despite my inner child's struggle to claim her voice as her own, she had always felt a deep and tremendous compassion for my mother's suffering, so much so that she took it upon herself to go on a mission, to fight for the mother whom she loved so much, and to fight for the voices of the family members that both my parents had lost.

The tragic result of this tremendous internal struggle was that my inner child ended up sacrificing her voice in order to take second place to my mother's voice and my mother's needs.

In the years that followed, the layers of these conflicting and turbulent emotions became the basis for the tapestry of my creative life and required constant expression in order for me to find some measure of peace within my own troubled heart.

And thus began the long and arduous journey towards my recovery from the agony of an inauthentic life, and the hard work of creating a life that would at last be in alignment with my true self.

Sonika Marcia Ozdoba

HEAVENLY FATHER
by Sonika Marcia Ozdoba

Heavenly Father, take my spirit,
And help me leave my weary heart behind,
It grieves within an aching body,
Longing to fly in freedom up high

Heavenly Father, raise my body,
And propel me from my hiding place,
To shatter the morning sky with brushstrokes
Like dawn's early goddess in urgent plight

Heavenly Father, take my soul
And throw my essence across your firmament
So I can leave my past and my pain
And live with you in eternal Light

Sonika Marcia Ozdoba

EXPLORING MY INNER WORLD

When it became clear, after the end of that season, that I would not be returning to my job in Zürich, my Chorus Director, Jürg Hämmerli, arranged for me to receive an "insurance salary" from the Opera House, which helped me stay afloat financially for three years before receiving my pension. By union law, if a chorus member was laid off for reasons of health, she would receive 90% of her salary for the first year and 80% of her salary for two years after that.

I was extremely fortunate that Zürich Opera House took such care of its employees well after their employment came to an end, in contrast to other countries where people were often laid off with no financial cushion to protect them in the interim between jobs. I will always be immensely thankful to my Chorus Director for his foresight and care during this very difficult and traumatic period of my life.

When I ultimately emigrated from Switzerland to the United States in 1995, I was allowed to take my pension money, which helped sustain me for a number of years and also helped me to start life in a new country.

After my return from India in September of 1993, I used the time to travel through Europe, in an attempt to get a better understanding of what had happened to me, and to heal the pain of all my losses.

In February of 1994, I became a disciple of Bhagwan Shree Rajneesh and joined the Bhagwan community of "sannyasins" (disciples) in Zürich, doing meditation and attending groups that addressed subjects as diverse as astrology, different schools of mysticism, and the dynamics in my family of origin.

But my inability to establish strong relationships, or feel a sense of belonging to anything, made it impossible to find real friendships within the sannyasin community, leaving me in a very lonely and isolated place.

I began the slow and painstaking work of making sense of my life in a way I had never done before. I wanted to explore and understand my highly complex inner life, and also find a way to process the life-changing and traumatic events I had experienced. In reviewing what had happened to me, I began to entertain the possibility that perhaps there was a different and much deeper perspective that I needed to gain.

For years after leaving the opera, I felt that God had abandoned and punished me by taking away what I loved most – my voice and my career. I would rage at Him for days and months, unable to accept the unfairness to which I was a witness, watching other friends in the profession enjoy enormous success, and not understanding why all I had worked for and treasured had been taken from me.

I was convinced that God was out to hurt me in every possible way. At the time, it was inconceivable to me that God might have had a very good reason for taking me out of the opera world at a time when I wanted so much to fulfill my lifelong dream of becoming a world-famous dramatic soprano.

As painful as it was, I had to take a hard and honest look at the realities of my profession and re-examine my very personal, emotional experience of life at the Opera. In order to come to peace with what had happened to me, I needed to get an understanding of the bigger picture.

Most people look at the world of opera and think it is exciting, glamorous and enviable. The truth behind that illusion is that the opera profession requires extremely hard physical work, long hours of standing, and hours of study and rehearsal time. The fierce competition makes it difficult to create true friendships, and I was often very lonely, even when surrounded by hundreds of people in a production.

Soloists need an excellent long-term memory to be able to memorize operas that they can sing at a moment's notice, and in the smaller opera houses, where "operettas" are sung, they are required to recite reams of dialogue in German, something I would have found impossible to do. Soloists also travel constantly and live out of hotels, trains and planes, which would have exhausted me.

In the Chorus, I had my daily routine, and if I was sick, other chorus members would cover for me. As a soloist, if you were ill, you still had to perform, or someone else would be called in to replace you. You would lose the job and the pay, something that would have caused me much anxiety.

Being an opera singer means that you give your whole life to your work. You sacrifice a normal life of balance for a life as a committed artist. You have to look after your health and your voice, and on those days where you have a demanding performance, you need to stay quiet and rest your vocal cords.

Because of your schedule, the theater becomes your only social life, and since I was unable to make friends there, for fear that they would find out about my illnesses, I felt lost, once the season was over, and found myself with no support system or social connections outside of the theater.

But for me the most difficult aspect of the profession was the very destructive manner in which people in the music business would treat one another. I saw emotional destructiveness in the theater on a level that so horrified my sense of decency and justice, that I knew I did not have the inner strength to deal with that kind of cruelty, without it affecting my health and spiritual wellbeing.

When all was said and done, the final and ultimate realization was that, in the same way that my hands and wrists were too weak for a concert pianist career, I was also not physically strong enough to take on the career of a dramatic soprano. When considering my physical build and my highly sensitive nervous system, both career choices would have been the wrong ones for me.

Today I know that a solo career in opera would have killed me within a week.

On a deeper level, the opera was taking me further and further away from my inner truth. The more roles I played on stage, the more disconnected I became from myself. The body is a voice and it constantly speaks to us. But at the time I was not listening or paying heed to its messages.

It kept screaming louder and louder, to get my attention, until it finally won the battle and I was forced to listen to what it had been trying to communicate to me for years.

The return of my battle with bulimia at this highly stressful time forced me to examine my relationship with my body. I had lived my whole life trying to free myself of my mother's shadow, to remove the "mask of the Holocaust" that had suffocated me for so many years.

Yet the child part of me was afraid that if I gave up the holocaust with my body, I would lose my connection with my mother. I believed that my mother would only love me if I empathized with her by making myself as miserable as she was, so I chose opera, with its plethora of tragic stories, as the perfect art form, to mirror her life. I had gone back to Europe hoping to find closure, for my own personal redemption, with the life events that had shaped her destiny.

The bulimia was the shell I created to protect myself from her toxic emotional influence during my early childhood experiences with her. But the irony was that her life story had left me terrified of being happy, because I was afraid it would betray all she had gone through.

As a result, I kept finding or putting myself in situations that ultimately brought me pain. It was a reflection of some kind of pattern – for example, enduring working with hostile coworkers, or taking self-destructive measures to comfort myself. My worth, on some level, came from staying in situations that caused me extreme pain.

I was emotionally entangled with my mother to such an extent that I had no idea whose life I was leading. I needed to separate from her, yet still stay connected to her, and this dilemma is what caused all the conflict. I did not know how to be Sonika, without my mother's dark cloud hanging over my life, and I wanted more than anything to feel like a success at something I had achieved, without her taking all the credit for me reaching that success.

I knew that it was my responsibility as an adult to learn how to mother myself and be kind to myself. But the wounds were so deep, and I was in such a spiritually dark place, that I needed a long period of time to really process all the feelings I had suppressed and allowed to fester inside of me.

My relationship with my mother had had the deepest and most debilitating effect on my life, and I needed time to free myself from her toxic influence.

In 1993, I went to an addiction treatment center in Holland for four and a half months, to address my problems with bulimia. My core inability to build strong relationships, as well as severe communication issues with the staff, ultimately led to my having to leave the center.

I had met a woman there who ended up taking me home with her to her family in Neuchâtel, in the French part of Switzerland. I lived there for three months, recovering from the trauma of the extreme and exhausting methods of emotional catharsis used at the addiction treatment center.

But there was no life for me in this beautiful, tiny French town and, in the end, my friend could not help me to build a new life. I was like a lost soul wandering in the desert with no connection to anyone or anything.

My life in Switzerland had come to an end, and the only solution I could see was to return to my family of origin in California, after thirteen years of being away from home.

Sonika Marcia Ozdoba

WATER
by Sonika Marcia Ozdoba

Water running like tears
Over the chambers of my soul
Healing me of past wounds
Leaving my heart as green pasture

Water flowing through my eyes
To make my sight anew
Washing away the filter
Of my imagined thoughts and pain

Water lifts me up
And helps me spread my wings
So that I can fly to God's heaven
And bathe in the dusk of the sky

Sonika Marcia Ozdoba

COMING HOME

Singing at the opera and doing solo concert work were all part of my search for authentic self-expression. But ultimately I needed to leave the world of "performing," and seeking love and approval from an audience, to rediscover what my true purpose was, and go on the arduous journey towards finding out what God wanted me to do with my life.

As I left my career behind me, and all the falsehood attached to being someone I was not, I wandered for a long time through the desert of my own uncertainty, wondering if I would ever find my true north.

Landing a good job in one of the top ten opera houses in Europe should have made me happy, but underneath it all, I felt that my whole career had been a lie, and I had to face the lie that I had perpetuated.

I had been an excellent and hardworking singer, but my technical ability had been limited, and I would never have sustained the solo career I had longed for. I was afraid people would find out about my lack of competence in certain aspects of my career, and I could not risk the humiliation of exposure. Deep down, I knew I had the potential to be a truly great artist, but it took leaving the profession to realize that I was in the wrong playing field.

There had also been many unaddressed personal problems that lay beneath the cultured, sophisticated image that I radiated to the outside world. In addition to my challenges with bulimia and epilepsy, there were also severe communication problems, social anxiety disorder, a variety of phobias, and a lifelong tendency towards obsessive compulsive behavior.

I was brought face to face with all these underlying issues and, once I left the Opera, I felt progressively more disconnected from people in general and the world as I knew it. I longed to find a resting place where my soul could explore and absorb the long sought-after answers to my questions.

With my career lying like an old shell on a dusty mantelpiece, I went into a numb and terrified paralysis. I had worn a mask for so long that I had no clue as to who I was underneath it. The mask had suffocated my true creativity and, most of all, my heart.

I felt suspended in time between two realities, the old one and the new one being born, with no one to guide me along the path. The mask had been the basis of my whole way of being and, without it, I had to build a new persona with no clue whatsoever as to my true identity or my true path in life.

Letting go of the "layers" left me with no anchor to hold on to, no rope to grasp, and no net to catch me. My spirit was exhausted from years of living a way of life totally out of sync with my natural rhythm and my innermost needs.

I had betrayed my own integrity without even knowing that it was missing, an integrity I had relinquished at such a young age, in order to survive, and now I desperately needed to find it again.

I had to let go of a whole way of being in the world, and at the same time accept the terror of being on an undefined road without a map. A silent terrified scream raged through my body and soul, but despite my constant prayers and pleas for guidance, I received no answers at the time.

It took me many years to discover that God had taken away a career I thought I had wanted. With his infinite wisdom and understanding, He had chosen exactly the right moment to remove me from a painfully inauthentic lifestyle and career that was costing me vital life energy and leaving me exhausted as a result.

What I initially perceived as punishment turned out to be the most extraordinary rescue mission. God stopped me, just in time, from heading in a direction that He knew would ultimately destroy my soul.

After packing up all my belongings in November 1995, I left Switzerland and went back to my family in California, to stay with my mother in her two-bedroom apartment in Palo Alto.

Two weeks after my arrival in the United States, I was hit by a car while walking across an intersection, tearing the ligaments in my left foot as I went sprawling onto the pavement.

It took over four months to recuperate and, in my extreme pain, I turned to music as the only resource that could heal my body and spirit. With a foot full of torn ligaments, I walked two and a half blocks each day to the Unity Church in Palo Alto, where I had received permission to use the piano in the sanctuary.

A new source of creativity had opened up for me through musical composition, and I poured all my energy into my composing work.

A friend had bought me a book of paintings by the American painter, Maxfield Parrish, and I became fascinated with the idea of setting his art work to music.

I started writing piano compositions that were inspired by his paintings, and later added the paintings and sculptures of other American artists to my composing work. In essence, I became what I call a "musical painter", attempting to "paint in sound" what I saw on the canvas or in the sculpture.

I scoured the art stores in Palo Alto for posters of art work that reflected some kind of spiritual message for me. Writing the music for these paintings gave me a kind of release from my physical and emotional pain.

I called this new art form "Sound-Painting" and began giving concerts of my original compositions, with posters of the artwork on display. It gave me a renewed sense of pleasure to communicate my process and my perspective to audiences, who responded very positively to my work. I felt that I was making a difference in people's lives with what I considered to be "pioneer work" in the field of art and spirituality, and was especially gratified to see how people were moved by the music I had written.

When I left the opera, I had lost my connection with audiences and had withdrawn from public life. My "Sound-Painting" work now filled a gaping void socially and creatively, and for three years I gave concerts of my piano pieces, original songs and "Sound-Paintings" throughout the Bay Area.

The music came pouring out of me like a dam that had opened its gates for all the water to flow through, without limits. I loved the combination of music and art, of sound and image, and began to really explore art as a kind of spiritual messenger.

People would ask me, "Sonika, how do you write music for a painting?"

The only reply I could think of was, "I just listen to the painting." The painting was a messenger for me. It forced me to listen to its message with my skin, with my whole body, with an alert but intense silence, and then write the music it inspired.

During my time at Unity Church, I met a videographer named Jim, who made videos of the sermons at the church each week. When he asked if I would like him to film my first concert there, I was thrilled to have someone to help me. Jim ended up assisting me with every aspect of my concert performances, including publicity, transporting the art work and recording the concert on video.

Jim once told me that one of my original songs entitled "She Walks the Night," had such an impact on him that he said to himself, "This woman needs to stay in the U.S. She has an important message for the world." And from that point on, he did everything he could to help me get that message out to my audiences.

Jim knew of the incredible losses I had suffered, and he was concerned that if I were to return to Europe, I would be completely alone and without support. His exact words were, "I was worried that, if you went back to Switzerland, you would jump off a bridge." That is most probably what I would have done.

So, in 1997, he asked me to marry him and we were married for eight years. His intention was to give me a chance to start again in a new country as well as a base from which to heal.

Although it was not an easy marriage, Jim was the one person I could always rely on, whenever I needed a real friend. For those eight years, he stood by me as a steady support, and I was extremely grateful to have a real partner to help me.

Jim helped me learn how to drive on the right hand side of the road. In Rhodesia, we had always driven on the left side of the road. One time I took a left hand turn into oncoming traffic in the left lane, where the cars were coming in my direction, and had to very swiftly change to the right lane! Not exactly a good way to "meet" people - head-on! Jim accompanied me on the freeways for two whole months before I had the courage to actually try driving on my own.

In 1998, we were offered the chance to run the apartment building where we lived in Mountain View, and we made friends with many of the tenants. In addition, I began teaching voice students at home and doing part time office work to make some money. Later that year, we went to an Art Expo in Los Angeles where I was approached by promoters of Richard Franklin's artwork to write a series of compositions in memory of the artist, who had recently died in a plane crash.

The Franklin project was the final composing project that I took on. My marriage was not going well at the time, and after I had performed the eleven "Sound-Painting" compositions at Santa Clara University, all inflow of musical ideas came to an abrupt halt and I could not hear the music any more.

I had smashed right into my second creative wall – the first time with the loss of my voice, and now with the disappearance of my composing ability. I felt that God was punishing me for the second time, and I could not endure another loss.

By this time, I was at a point where no explanation made sense to me. I kept asking God to show me a way out of this unbearable agony, but He provided me with no answers to my questions.

Being a creative artist had always meant the freedom to do what I loved, but hitting a wall for the second time in my creative life left me at a loss as to what to do next. I felt I was dealing with something so huge and so baffling that I was unable to grasp the extent and severity of what was happening to me.

I lost my connection to my heart and became a shadow of myself, going through the motions of life, yet feeling nothing but a sense of numbness.

What followed was a period of seven excruciating years of chronic depression. The only thing that saved me from suicide was the discovery of art therapy and the long-awaited re-emergence of my inner child.

TURN YOUR EYES
by Sonika Marcia Ozdoba

Turn your eyes inward
And seek your answers there
In the silence of your silence
Where your stillness lies so fair

Turn your eyes to your heart
Where all your answers lie
In the dormant room so hidden
Of your thoughts that pass on by

Turn your eyes from the darkness
And behold your inner light
That you have hidden from yourself
Bring it forth, back from the night

Sonika Marcia Ozdoba

EMERGENCE OF A NEW LANGUAGE

I feel very fortunate that I had my family in California when I arrived because they were there to help me, especially after my accident. Many immigrants had come to the United States with no one to help them. I felt very lucky to have my family and Jim to be there as a support to me in every way.

Since Jim and I were now managing our apartment building, we were able to live rent-free, which was an extraordinary gift in view of the enormously high rentals in Mountain View. We had a beautiful two-bedroom apartment which I was able to furnish with part of my pension money from Switzerland. The walls were decorated with the artwork from my "Sound-Paintings", and I was able to open a voice teaching studio at home.

I would spend my mornings helping Jim look after the property, and I actually enjoyed this kind of work because it enabled me to work with my hands and create order in my home environment.

Working with my hands is something I inherited from my father who had been a tailor by trade and who used to make uniforms for the British army in Rhodesia. He specialized in what he called "invisible mending", where he would leave no traces of any holes on the clothing that he repaired.

I inherited his attention to detail, and it reminded me of a "Channeling" workshop in France which I had attended during my travels in Europe. After completing the course, a fellow-participant noticed me packing up my belongings. "You leave a place as though you had never been there – you don't even leave a cigarette in the ashtray."

His comment stayed with me for a long time and made me wonder why I was so careful about hiding any trace of having been present in that room.

My friend had sensed a deeper reason and mystery behind my behavior.

Perhaps it was an echo of my parents having been through the war and having to leave no traces behind that would give away clues to the German soldiers looking for evidence of their presence.

It seems that the pattern of behavior had been passed on unconsciously from parent to child – I learned to never leave evidence that would point to my existence.

At times, I felt suspended in time between two generations, hanging on to a past that was not mine, but one which had directed my own course of history and led me to do things that took me literally years to understand. While remembering my father's trade and his love for invisible mending, I felt that it had now become my task to unravel the tapestry of my own baffling behavior patterns that had become such a ritual in my everyday life.

I had used my hands to create beautiful works of art through my piano pieces and musical compositions. But what my hands had created also held the essence of what those hands concealed, and they now needed to reveal what was hidden beneath their creation.

My father had sought to cover and eradicate the holes in the suits he repaired.

For me, however, the holes in my own history needed mending.

When my mother became too old to live on her own, we packed up her apartment in Palo Alto and took her to live in the cottage behind my sister's house.

In the last years of her life, she became more fragile and needy of having her children nearby. Even though we had never had a good relationship, she would ask me, time and again, when I was coming to visit her.

My sense was that my mother was trying to make up for a lot of the pain she felt she had caused me, and she wanted to leave me well provided for. Two months before she passed away, she asked my brother-in-law to buy me a new car so that I would be safe on the road.

The "Wiedergutmachungsgeld" (literally meaning, "money to make good again"), was a kind of "allowance" sent by the German government to survivors of the Holocaust, as "reparation costs" after the war.

It was extremely poignant to me that my mother had saved this money to help pay for my car and had never spent any of it on herself, despite all the suffering she had endured.

But for me it was particularly heart-wrenching that I was now receiving this "reparation" after the war – her war and mine…

Shortly before she died, Mom asked me to promise her something.

She said, "Promise me that you will never give up your music and your art, because one day, your music and your art will save your life."

She understood how important it was for me to keep using my creativity, no matter how difficult life became.

That car kept me safe on the road for eleven years, but her words were truly the legacy that she had left me, and they made me realize that she knew me better than I had ever given her credit for.

When my mother finally passed away, I learned that a trust fund had been established, that helped me survive for many years after her death. She had asked my brother-in-law to look after the money and, as always, he was faithful to her wishes and helped me with stewardship of the money. I was truly grateful for her foresight and for the financial cushion that she provided. It gave me time to heal, and time to sort out a new direction for my life.

Many years previously, I had taken up painting, in an attempt to make visible the "block" inside my own psyche, and in 1997 found an art therapy class which completely changed my life. Art therapy deals with one's inner language of images, and I discovered that I was a very

THE SOUL WITH TWO VOICES

different person on the inside to the person that I projected on the outside. The language of images spoke to me and at last I felt that my inner child now had a language through which she could communicate with me.

I worked in various different mediums – painting, clay, drawing, and collage – and was able to express long-hidden feelings through the artwork. I discovered an ability to "read" people's emotions through their art work, which became a kind of window for me to see into their emotional world.

There were some opportunities available to facilitate classes for teenagers and women's groups, but nothing that provided me with any form of steady income. Primarily, I ended up doing art therapy for myself and found it to be extremely useful.

Performing is often a distraction from one's inner world. Now I had the time to focus on what was happening on an internal level, beneath the image I had constructed of a calm, educated woman who seemed to have her life under control, and who appeared to be unperturbed by life's challenges.

What I discovered through art therapy is that this outer image was indeed a well-constructed lie, for it masked deep sadness, insecurity and a heart that was constantly at war with itself.

There was little in my life that brought me real joy, and I often felt lifeless and empty, like a bare canvas, with nothing painted on it. I felt like I was wandering in a hollow silent glade where no one could find me, lost underneath all the unspoken expectations of family and the people in my life.

The creative child inside me had retreated to an invisible place where she could cease to exist and just be quiet with the few things that made her happy. After I closed up everything to do with music, she found refuge and sanctuary in the dark confines of my subconscious mind.

The child part of me had gotten lost beneath the roles I had played for so many years. I felt conscious of the need to be a "responsible" adult, but something fundamental was missing in my life. The little girl inside was miserable and had been for a very long time. With art, my inner child found a place where she could be a child again, express herself and be happy.

I discovered through art therapy that my happiness depended strongly on my connection with my inner child, and the canvas became the vehicle for the adult woman in me to discover through imagery what my inner child needed.

At this time, I became aware of the disturbing truth that I lived with a complete split in my own personality. It felt like two distinct people inside my body. The one had everything under control and was meticulous in her habits. The other was like a wild raging animal completely out of control.

The tension between these two personalities became so intense, and their battle for supremacy so loud, that my only way to deaden their concurrent need to be heard was by consuming excess food and using large amounts of laxatives to wash their voices out of my body.

What fascinated me was that these two personalities were completely unaware of each other and oblivious as to when "the other one" was going to take over. I knew that my family had no idea about the times when my mind slipped into two people, or when I became unconscious of the passage of time. There were days when I could not leave the apartment, when the exhaustion from this internal battle became so overwhelming that I would need to sleep for hours.

Luckily, I had developed a habit of writing down all the things I accomplished every day. Once events went into the past, it was as though my mind put a veil across those events, and I was unable to remember anything from one day to the next. I would have to check my daily calendar constantly. I had no idea what had caused this condition, but I kept track of my life by writing things down.

I went back to performing for a short while, but a point came where I felt so betrayed by the world that I made the choice to shut down the music completely.

All my life, I had shared my musical talent with people who responded to my contribution by using, abusing and criticizing me. There came a moment where I made the final decision that enough was enough. I made a promise to myself that never again would the world profit from my gifts as a musician or be given the license to hurt me with my own God-given abilities.

After fifty years of giving my musical talents to the world, I finally took all of my recordings, concert videos and music tapes and threw every last trace of my musical career into the garbage. The feeling of relief and happiness from that one act was indescribable. I felt like I had thrown out a life that had brought me nothing but misery.

That small, fragile and powerless child, who had been unable for so long to defend her tiny and vulnerable self, had come out like a raging lion and used her hands to throw out everything that had caused her pain. The turtle shell that had weighed her down for so many years was finally lifted and thrown off her back with the most intense and overpowering rage.

With that one act of throwing out every last vestige of my musical life, I set my inner child free, and finally gave her permission to have her own dream.

OYSTER WITH A PEARL
by Sonika Marcia Ozdoba

She hides her pearl
So no one can see
Afraid to trust
Afraid to be

Caught in the web
Of her tiny heart
Afraid to break open
Afraid to start

To break the shell
Is what she must do
Leave the shell behind
Is the only way through

Sonika Marcia Ozdoba

END OF AN ERA

In April of 2005, I made the decision to leave my marriage and give Jim a chance to find a true partner in life. We had both been unhappy for a long time and it was time for me to take responsibility for my own part in the breakdown of the marriage. Jim was not my problem – I was. I needed to stand on my own two feet and find out where I was going with my life.

I found a one-bedroom apartment around the corner from where we lived. The first month was the toughest. I was terrified of being alone and used to come back to Jim's apartment in the evenings just to sit with him and talk, or watch television, because I could not face being alone.

With time, however, I slowly began building a new life and started up my voice teaching business again in the new apartment. I made friends at my building and got into recovery for my eating disorder. It had always amazed me how Jim was so comfortable with being alone. He had a wide range of interests and was constantly watching programs on current affairs, politics and history. He was an avid reader and had knowledge in many different areas.

In the beginning, I missed our interesting discussions, and having someone to talk to, but slowly life took on its own rhythm and I was able to extricate myself from my attachment to him. Jim had kept his commitment to help me to start a new life for myself, but it was time now for me to move on.

After a few years, I moved to a new apartment nearby, but within a short time, the rents were raised to such an astronomical level that I was unable to afford such tremendous costs. I applied for low-income housing and was told that it could take up to five years to get accommodation at one of their facilities.

Two months after my application, I received a phone call notifying me that a studio apartment in Mountain View was available. The call came at the same time that my rent was about to be raised by $300 a month, a sheer miracle that only God could have orchestrated.

Right before I moved, I went to Kaiser Hospital in Santa Clara to have my heart tested with an electrocardiogram (EKG) and was informed by the nurse that I was due for a mammogram. Normally I had my mammograms done at Kaiser Hospital in Mountain View and I promised the nurse that I would go the following week. She was absolutely insistent that I go immediately after the EKG. Jokingly, I commented that I would do it as a favor to her, and obeyed her instructions.

One week later, the results of the mammogram showed that I had stage zero breast cancer and needed to have a lumpectomy. Had I not listened to that nurse, and waited another few weeks, the cancer would have spread and become far more serious. It was yet another example of how God had intervened at a time when I needed Him most. I made a point of sending a referral to that nurse's supervisor, informing her how that nurse had saved my life. Without her being so serious about doing her job well, I could have been faced with a mastectomy or lost my life to breast cancer.

Shortly after the surgery, I sold most of my furniture, packed up my few basic belongings and moved to my new studio apartment. I was extremely lucky that all four apartments where I had lived were in walking distance of one another in Mountain View, so moving from one apartment to another fortunately did not involve large costs or distances.

The facility and the location of my new apartment were ideal for everything I needed. I was close to all the shops, grocery stores, parks and libraries that I frequented, and was able to save a lot of money by living there.

It was a great relief to at last live in a place where I had far more contact with other tenants, in comparison to other buildings where I had lived.

My studio apartment was almost like a child's room and it struck me as deliciously ironic that, after throwing out all my music and an inauthentic lifestyle, I now had a home where my inner child could have exactly what she needed to express herself, be it through art or writing.

There was a bed, a small kitchen table with two chairs, a computer station, a perfect size kitchen and bathroom, and enough closet space for my clothes. The simplicity of my lifestyle was ideal for my basic needs and I was able to keep things extremely functional and easy to manage.

After settling into the apartment, I went back to Kaiser for six weeks of radiation treatment at the Cancer Treatment Center. Over several months I completed a project of eleven three-dimensional collages using masks, in an attempt to "unmask the self" through art. But once all the collages were finished, the medium no longer appealed to me and I began to turn my attention more to my writing and my recovery.

I took some time to look back on my prolific creative life as a singer, pianist, composer, arranger, recording artist, musical painter, art form inventor, and visual artist. There had been a massive outpouring of creativity in all these different arenas. Yet suddenly I stood at a crucial turning point, where none of those mediums spoke to me anymore.

I had chosen to be a creative channel, an instrument for God to use, but ironically it was the relationship with God and with myself that I most needed to find.

The only way forward, as I saw it, was to "unload the truck", so to speak, of all the emotional baggage that I had been carrying for so many years, and write my story so that I could see a clear way through to the other side.

I cleaned out my environment of any old documents, books and other possessions that I no longer needed. My former identity as a musician had been put to rest, and I said goodbye to my old life. The shell of my old identity had been cast to the wind and all that was left was a pile of dead leaves at the foot of an oak tree.

My world became strangely silent. The telephone was still. I felt as though I were in a state of incubation, wrapped in the silence of the womb, where no one could reach me. And from this safe and invisible place, I shed the outworn skin that had entrapped my real self for so long.

This shedding process continued for several years, as I let go of connections and attachments to people and places that no longer resonated with the person I was becoming. Like a mother, who cannot see but only feel the growth of a new baby in her belly, I could feel a fundamental change in the roots of my soul, but could not see the depth at which it was happening.

I watched the invisible changes occurring in nature, and tried not to be sad at my old self dying and falling away like a winter making way for spring. My life had always felt like a continuous process of death and rebirth, and somehow I sensed that this is what it would probably always be like – everything had its season, and it was time to let it go and allow new seed to emerge.

Throughout this process, my family was extremely helpful to me and I was truly grateful for their support. As the artist in the family, I had always forged a unique path through life, searching for my own truth and direction, and it had often been difficult for them to understand my need to take an unconventional road. Even when the journey was difficult and lonely, I continued with my quest, as any spiritual warrior must do, to discover the answers that I needed to find.

Life continued in its beautiful and gentle way, and I watched with pleasure as my older sister's children and grandchildren were growing up. But I knew that my path would always lead me in a different direction, guided by this constant process of change so beautifully reflected in the seasons. I had left my family a long time ago, and had returned to find out that they were still there for me, with all their love, in spite of my having believed otherwise, for so many years.

I found myself at a stage of life where there was only love and gratitude for all that they had made possible for me. I was grateful to my mother for her help after she passed on, and I deeply appreciated the ever-present help and care that my family gave to me. It was a relief to discover that I no longer needed the façade I had lived with for so long. I could finally just be myself and be true to what brought me peace and joy.

Many times I battled with my faith and asked God what new mission He wanted me to fulfill at this stage of life. The message I received in the quiet hours with Him was not about fulfilling anything at all. He wanted me just to be constantly in relationship with Him, stay close to Him at all times, and keep growing in wisdom, experience and love. I came to accept that all the people he had sent into my life were mirrors and teachers from whom I had important lessons to learn.

We live in a loving universe with forces that only want to enhance our lives with the best possible opportunities.

What I came to realize after so many years was that it was my own distorted perception of people and events that had colored my whole experience of life. And this perceptual falsehood was based on all the erroneous beliefs that I had held since childhood.

By examining these distortions of perception, I could finally see how the negative beliefs and the stories that I told myself about the people in my life had caused all my misery, and I could finally start to let those beliefs go. It freed me up to see that it was my responsibility to remove those distortions in my thinking, and to see the truth.

Essentially, we all see what we choose to see, often believing our own negative projections. It was now time to change that perception, and look at the world through a different set of eyes. For a time, involvement in the music world had brought me joy and fulfillment, but when I lost the joy in my work, I needed to walk away from it.

After many years of searching for answers, I realized that losing my voice had compelled me to find the one thing that was missing – my inner silence and my connection to God – the core of what I needed more than anything else.

And the only way that I found that light was by going into the darkness. Whenever there was a winter in my spirit, I needed to go back to the earth to await new growth.

I brought myself to the table with pen and paper to face the final confrontation – the one with myself. And the battle that raged was only there when I forgot that God was by my side, and had always been there.

When my mind would wander to that lonely place on my inner seashore that was strewn with pebbles of fear and self-doubt, it reminded me to keep moving ahead, work hard, and take the next right action, even when I had no idea where I was headed.

I am proud of all that I risked and accomplished, yet that little girl inside me is sometimes still vulnerable and afraid, and she often forgets that love surrounds her at all times in a troubled and unstable world.

The one factor that has been a constant has been the search for what is true for me. I have learned much from many teachers and different schools of thought, but in the end, life has been my ultimate teacher, and taking the "road less travelled" has and continues to be a beautiful journey, full of wonder, mystery and endless surprise.

WALK WITH ME
by Sonika Marcia Ozdoba

Walk with me, gentle spirit of my soul
And guide each step in my journey forth
Be my path as I step toward the sun
And warm my heart as I head north

Walk with me, O fire of my stride
And take me to places I have never been
Light the staircase that lies in shadows
And show me treasures I have never seen

Walk with me, O love of my life
Toward the cliffs about my ocean of tears
Stay close to me and keep me warm
Side by side through the valley of years

Sonika Marcia Ozdoba

TO THE ARTISTS OF THE WORLD

As I approach the closing chapters of my book, I feel compelled to share my message with those artists who are striving to make their own voices heard.

I know from personal experience the nature of your struggle with yourselves, and the deep conflicts you deal with. I honor the intense amount of work and sacrifice you have given, to make your mark upon the world. And I can empathize with the pain and suffering that accompany the difficult choices you are constantly challenged to face.

As artists, you have been called to take on the mission of this difficult path, one that is filled with joy and creativity, but also with heart-wrenching moments and many dark nights of the soul.

You have been called upon to do a special work in this life.

This is your assignment, the path God has chosen for you.

On this long, perilous journey through the mountains, you will be challenged to express your truth with no question of compromise. You must carry with you a golden scepter, to separate with one clean cut what is true and what is untrue, what is real and what is fantasy, what is authentic and what does not resonate with your being.

You must move beyond the veil, beyond the anxiety, beyond your fear. Listen to the signals from your body, and your instincts, and always move to higher ground.

Cut through to the deep well of your own wisdom that is buried in the rivers and the streams of your inner life. When in doubt, listen to the sounds of the water, listen to the vibration of the wind, and feel that wind in your soul.

It is your God-given right to challenge all established ways of thinking and to express everything you carry in your heart. For your heart is a place you can trust, a place within from which God can lead you.

God has entrusted each one of you with a sacred contract that only you can fulfill, and every step of the way, He will test your commitment and perseverance.

But, if you hold to that blazing light, that fire that burns away the dross of inauthenticity, you will be blessed with the ecstatic happiness of an eagle soaring in flight, claim mastery of the sky, and be free to reach as high as your wings will take you.

You will see a vision of your life without self-imposed limitations, fueled by the ever-present fire of your unique brand of creativity, and the knowledge that you have stayed faithful to the quest.

You will face many baffling situations and much inner turmoil, and it may take years to see the thread that runs like a river through your life experiences.

But along the way, you will come to a much deeper understanding of the complexities within your own heart, for the path of the artist is one of self-mastery, and it requires the continual conquest of your own limited thinking and perception.

Each one of you has a unique form of self-expression that the world needs to hear and witness. Your journey of life will be the journey back to your own voice and your very special way of expressing that voice.

The love inside your heart will be your guide, but the fire in your soul is what will get you there.

And I know, for certain, that God in all His mercy will be waiting eagerly as you pick up the challenge. He will guide and protect you, at every junction in the road, the same way that He has guided and protected me, and will extend His loving arms to embrace you as true children of the Light.

At the end of your journey, the one thing I can promise and assure you of is this –

You will reach the Promised Land when you have been faithful to yourself.

Sonika Marcia Ozdoba

FACES

by Sonika Marcia Ozdoba

Faces within faces
An eternal cycle
Till you get to the original face
The one without the layers
Of all you have built over it –
All that protects you,
All that shields you from life,
From all that you feel –
And the universe, in its infinite wisdom,
Smiling, knowing, and always beckoning you
To take the risk –
To drop all that you know,
All that you see,
All that you believe is real –
To find your heart,
For in your heart is your original face.

Sonika Marcia Ozdoba

MY DREAM

Writing the story of my spiritual journey and what I learned along the way has been a dream of mine for a long time. In this memoir, I chose to focus on my personal feelings about my life, rather than emphasize the external events, and to outline the development of who I became as a result of those experiences.

It is my hope, through telling my story from a very personal and deeply emotional place, that I have shown how even the most difficult internal challenges can be overcome, and that true freedom is attainable, when you make the commitment to finding your own voice and speaking your truth.

In telling my story to you, my reader, I wanted to show that it is possible to move from sadness to joy, to choose happiness instead of resignation, and to move from feeling powerless to being powerful. I wanted you to know with full certainty that it is never too late to reclaim your life, by taking the time to listen to your inner child, whose voice so desperately needs to be heard.

My dream is that the words of my message to the world will resonate in your soul, give you hope and courage, and be a shining torch for the forgotten and neglected corners of your own heart.

I hope you will be moved by my passion for the truth, as I feel and experience it, and that my words will encourage you to take action on your own behalf, and to move towards all that brings you joy.

In writing this memoir, my only desire has been to fulfill my sacred contract with God, and I pray that He is pleased with the work of art I have created out of my own life. By opening my heart so wide, I pray that the healing that is channeled through my words will cause you to stop in your tracks and feel the impact of God's glory.

And finally, it is my hope that you who read my story will take the time to listen to your inner child, take her by the hand, and go dancing with her into the Light.

THE LILAC TREES

In concluding this memoir, I would like to go back in time to a childhood incident which happened while growing up in Rhodesia. When I was twelve years old, I would ride my bike to school every day through a stretch of road lined on both sides with magnificent, tall jacaranda trees, whose lilac blossoms stretched overhead like lovers extending their beauty to one another, creating a canopy that would momentarily shut out the sunlight.

The trees would drop their lilac blossoms on the road beneath, almost as a token of love for one another, creating a wedding carpet of lilac. I would ride my bike at the speed of lightning down that road, and feel the wind through my long and lustrous brown hair, sensing even at that young age that this is what heaven must feel like. I felt as if God and I were riding side by side on my bike and felt happy and content just to be enveloped by so much delicious color and beauty.

This vivid memory of the lilac trees came back to me later in life as part of a vision for my last years on earth.

I imagined that one day I would meet my soulmate, and share the last years of my life with him in a beautiful valley, together with all the people I cherished in our community of kindred spirits.

When the day of my departure drew near, I would say goodbye to all those who had been such an integral part of my life, and walk with my partner to the top of the hill overlooking the valley. We would spend our last evening together, watching the sunset, and my heart would be filled with love and gratitude for all we had shared.

When I knew it was time to go, I would embrace him for the last time, knowing we would see each other again soon. With a beautiful smile on his face, he would walk down the hill, and wave goodbye to me.

I would stay at the top of that hill, enveloped in deep silence, meditating on the scene in front of me. With a serene and happy heart, I would be filled with the knowledge that I had accomplished what I came here to do, and at the same time be filled with excitement at the prospect of going home.

There would be a deep sense of belonging as well as the desire to break free and become one with God again – free of my body and free of any constraints. When the moment came, my spirit would leave my body and begin to travel upwards, moving ever faster towards the tunnel leading to the other side...

Before long I would be racing through that beautiful tunnel of lilac, just like that twelve-year-old had raced on her bike through the canopy of jacaranda trees.

I would smell their wonderful fragrance, and feel that carpet of soft and delicate blossoms beneath my feet.

And as the end of the tunnel approached, the Light would suddenly hit my face with an intense force, and my spirit would be shattered into a thousand pieces all over the sky.

I would know a racing thrill in my soul that I had never imagined possible, the ecstasy of being a part of the entire universe, a part of every cloud in the firmament.

I would look down and see my beloved waving his hand at the sky, knowing I had made it to the other side, and had become part of the light shining down on him. He would stare pensively into the setting sun, wistful that I was no longer by his side, but also happy I was home, knowing he would join me when it was time for him to leave.

And with a quiet sense of pleasure, he would see my smile permeating the clouds, and would feel my love for him pouring out of the sunlight.

We would hold each other in that moment of sheer joy, before I went flying further and further towards the Light, like a happy child on a bicycle.

Sonika Marcia Ozdoba

LILAC-COLORED SILENCE
by Sonika Marcia Ozdoba

Lilac sky and earth shimmering with the evening glow
Light above and below, the sunset enveloping
The mountains and stones of my rock-solid being
Drawing to me all that is heaven-made and natural
All that has stood there since time immemorial
The mystery of creation in all its peaceful wonder
Majestic and demanding an awestruck silence
My inner being in harmony with the vastness of that ocean
And constant as the stones that bear
The brunt of eroding waters

When all is said and done, this is what shall remain
Of the earth and of my being
The memory of lilac-colored silence
My favorite color and my most authentic state of being
It all comes down to connecting with my inner world
And the intense pleasure
Of cool water encircling my sand-drenched feet
How I long to be walking in that magical, natural place
Surrounded by the beauty and stillness
Of this earth's ever-changing colors
Yet lilac is, for some strange reason
Where I feel most at home
Connected beyond this world
To other worlds in my distant memory

The water is my source and the rocks my salvation
And what joins them with a magic thread is the Light
Revealing and reflecting the colors
Of my heart and my happiness
There walks God in His majesty and infinite stillness
Bound to the earth like two lovers holding hands
The Alpha and Omega - as above, so below
In perfect balance and harmony
Listening beyond time and space
The sounds of light, joining all parts of existence
My lilac immersion into a sea of peace

This is where I found my lover, walking by the ocean wide
This is where I found my true heart, standing by my side
This is where God revealed his heart to me and I hear his call
This is where He revealed my essence
So that I could stand ten feet tall
This is where I have come to rest
Relieved at last of all my woes
This is where I shall stand forever,
To watch where the wind blows

Love your life, with both the rocks and the sea
Find your true heart, the same way God found me

ABOUT THE AUTHOR

Sonika Ozdoba is a creative artist, writer and musician, who was born in Zimbabwe, and who worked as a professional classical musician in South Africa, London and Switzerland.

After a 17-year career in opera and concert work, a life-changing spiritual experience forced her to move away from voice as an entertainment medium, and to search for the voice of her forgotten inner child, through the media of visual art and writing.

In this memoir, Sonika shares deeply personal insights from her career, and examines the lessons she learned along the way.

You can reach Sonika through the following email address:

sonikaozdoba@gmail.com